ROUGH CUT
WOODWORKING WITH TOMMY MAC

13 ALL-NEW PROJECTS FROM SEASON 2

TOMMY MACDONALD
WITH LAURIE DONNELLY

The Taunton Press

The Taunton Press
Inspiration for hands-on living®

The Taunton Press, Inc., 63 South Main Street, PO Box 5506
Newtown, CT 06470-5506
e-mail: tp@taunton.com

Editor: **SCOTT GIBSON**
Copy Editor: **CANDACE B. LEVY**
Indexer: **JAY KREIDER**
Interior design: **NICK CARUSO**
Layout: **AMY BERNARD RUSSO**
Illustrator: **CHRISTOPHER MILLS**
Photographer: **ANTHONY TIUELI, WGBH**
Photographer's Assistant: **LUCIO LECCE**

Library of Congress Cataloging-in-Publication Data in progress

ISBN 978-1-60085-821-5

Printed in the United States of America
10 9 8 7 6 5 4 3 2 1

For Rough Cut—Woodworking with Tommy Mac television show

Host: **THOMAS J. MACDONALD**
Executive Producer & Director: **LAURIE DONNELLY**
Senior Program Producer: **ANNE ADAMS**
Producers: **THOMAS J. MACDONALD, LAURIE DONNELLY, ANNE ADAMS**
Technical Advisor: **ELI CLEVELAND**
Editorial Consultant: **STEVE BROWN, CABINET AND FURNITURE MAKING
DEPARTMENT, NORTH BENNET STREET SCHOOL**
Director of Photography: **JOHN BAYNARD**
Audio: **JOHN O'CONNOR**
Online Editor: **DAVE ALLEN**
Assistant Editor: **JOE HEADRICK**
Music: **DAVID MASHER & CRIT HARMON**
Graphics: **BRUCE WALKER, ALISON KENNEDY, DAVID MASHER & INVERSION MEDIA**
Make-up: **ELIZABETH MOON**
National Marketing: **PETER PANAGOPOULOS, TARA RAFIEYMEHR PETTINATO,
JESSICA HARTZELL**
Station Relations: **NANCY BOCCHINO, VICTORIA YUEN**
© WGBH EDUCATIONAL FOUNDATION 2011

ABOUT YOUR SAFETY

Working wood is inherently dangerous. Using hand or power tools improperly or ignoring safety practices can lead to permanent injury or even death. Don't try to perform operations you learn about here (or elsewhere) unless you're certain they are safe for you. If something about an operation doesn't feel right, don't do it. Look for another way. We want you to enjoy the craft, so please keep safety foremost in your mind whenever you're in the shop.

To everyone who has ever been inspired to pick up a piece of wood and make something beautiful, memorable, and meaningful to you.

ACKNOWLEDGMENTS

Taunton Press

We'd like to start with a double shout out to The Taunton Press and the *Fine Woodworking* team, whose shared vision, hard work, and dedication help make our *Rough Cut* companion book possible. This includes thanks to editor Scott Gibson, art director Alison Wilkes, photo editor Erin Giunta, photographer Anthony Tiueli, photography assistant Lucio Lecce, layout artist Amy Russo, and illustrator Christopher Mills. And an extra special thanks to senior managing editor Carolyn Mandarano, whose vigilance helped take our series from the television screen to the pages you are now reading. We're proud to be associated with such a talented and dedicated group of people.

Thanks also to all the *Fine Woodworking* magazine staff, including group publisher Anatole Burkin, editor Asa Christiana, art director Michael Pekovich, and senior editor Matt Kenney, who have been supportive of Tommy since he started his woodworking career.

Our Funders

We also extend our deepest gratitude to our funders, without whom there would be no *Rough Cut— Woodworking with Tommy Mac.* Topping the list is Woodcraft. Many thanks to Sam Ross, Jeff Forbes, Jody Garrett, Dawn Knowst, Liz Byers, Vic Lombard, and Woodcraft's extended corporate team.

We also wish to thank all of the independent Woodcraft franchise owners who have graciously invited us into their stores and made us feel at home everywhere from Boston to Seattle.

Our Show Team

They are many people behind the scenes who help bring a show to air. A special thanks to our WGBH family, whose endless commitment and dedication is truly the driving force that makes our series an ongoing success. Among them, hats off to Anne Adams, Melissa Hench Adams, Karen Carroll Bennett, David Bernstein, Margaret Drain, Melissa Martin, Ariam McCrary, and all of our marketing and station relations team who help make our vision a reality.

With us in the sawdust trenches are Eli Cleveland, Steve Brown, John Baynard, John O'Connor, Dave Allen, David Masher, Elizabeth Mood, Ken Fishkin, and Jay Fialkov, who keep things looking great and running smoothly. Thanks also to all of our special on-air guests who have shared their talents, even under the most extreme conditions (as when the shop reached 110°F and everyone continued to keep their cool).

To Tommy's alma mater, the North Bennet Street School, thanks to those who help guide the integrity and accuracy of all of our projects.

And to those who were the focus of our *Rough Cut* Road Trips, thanks for sharing your unique worlds and expertise with audiences all across the country.

Our Families

Finally, thanks to our families. Tommy wishes to thank his entire family for keeping his feet on the ground and his ego in check. He also thanks his in-laws, especially his mother-in-law, Marsha, and his better half, his wife Rachel, who is a source of inspiration and unwavering support.

Laurie wishes to thank her ever-patient husband, Bill, and daughters, Katherine and Lydia, who have learned that if you marry or are born into the life of a television producer, things are never dull, are ever changing, and are a good source of comic relief. Laurie also wishes to remember her late dog, Baxter, the basset hound who was always there for her, even on the most challenging days.

Thanks team! Onward and upward.

Tommy and Laurie

CONTENTS

INTRODUCTION

Woodworking satisfies the soul. It allows you to make something out of nothing, whether you are creating a project for yourself or to give as a gift.

The projects in this companion book to the second season of *Rough Cut—Woodworking with Tommy Mac* were designed specifically to help you continue growing as a woodworker. You can build these projects just as they are or make them your own, as we say on our television show. We strongly suggest you work from the plans, but adapt them to make the project fit your home, your style, and your tastes. You'll find a few design options throughout this book to help you get started thinking about the projects in different ways.

As with the companion book to the first season of *Rough Cut,* tips and techniques are scattered throughout the book, all to help you develop your skills and get comfortable in the shop. The projects here have been designed to get you in the shop and have some fun. As always, be safe and remember that we encourage you to play around with these projects. Change them however you like to make them your own.

DRESSING MIRROR

Making Finger Joints on a Tablesaw

This cherry dressing mirror was inspired by the work of two brothers, Charles and Henry Greene, who were among the leaders of the Arts and Crafts movement in the United States. They were not only architects but also talented furniture designers, known for the unique details they incorporated into their work.

Several of their most noted details are focal points of this project: the interlocking finger joints featured on the case and the drawer; the cloud-lift pattern accentuating the top of the mirror; and the black ebony plugs. Together, these details contribute to the overall feel that people have come to associate with Greene and Greene design.

The finger joints are the real technical challenge of this project, but a simple technique developed by Steve Brown of the North Bennet Street School will allow you to make the joints quickly and accurately on a tablesaw.

We chose to make the dressing mirror out of cherry and the accent plugs out of ebony because Greene and Greene commonly used the two woods together. We learned from our *Rough Cut* Road Trip, though, that they were open to using all species of wood, so feel free to use whatever strikes your fancy.

To complete this project, you'll also need a few hardware store supplies, including a mirror, a length of threaded rod, drawer knobs, and a small piece of 1/4-in. cherry plywood for the back of the mirror.

Dressing Mirror

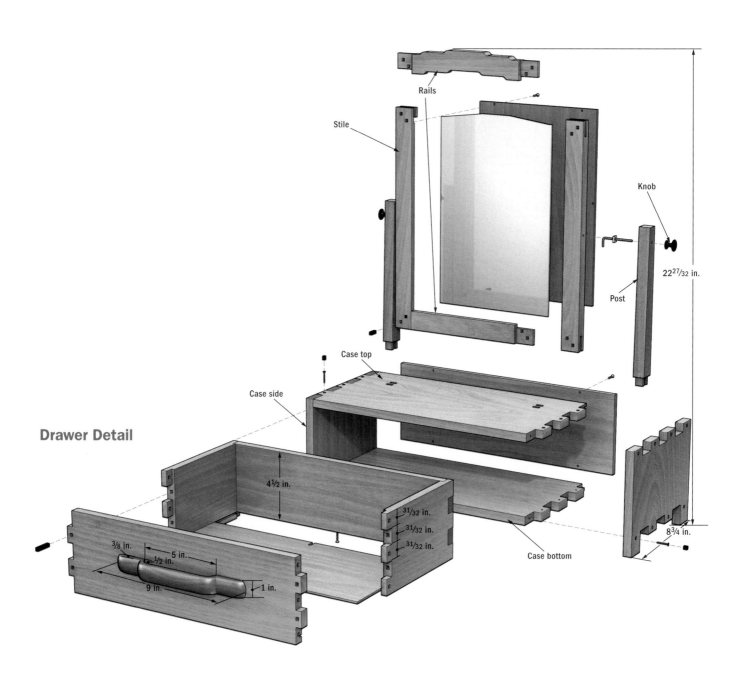

Rails

Stile

Knob

22$^{27}/_{32}$ in.

Post

Case top

Case side

Drawer Detail

4$^{1}/_{2}$ in.

3$^{1}/_{32}$ in.
3$^{1}/_{32}$ in.
3$^{1}/_{32}$ in.

Case bottom

8$^{3}/_{4}$ in.

$^{3}/_{8}$ in.

5 in.

$^{1}/_{2}$ in.

9 in.

1 in.

Mirror Frame

Frame Tenon

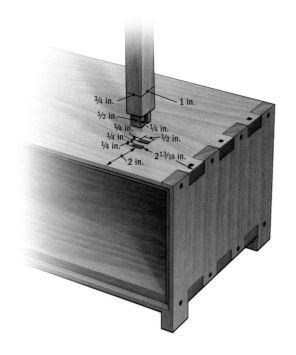

Rail and Drawer Pull

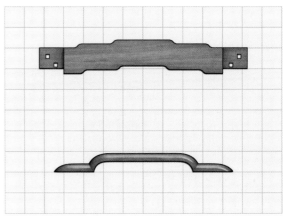

1 square = 1 in.

POWER TOOLS

Bandsaw
Cordless drill
Jointer
Mortising machine
Planer
Router
Router table
Tablesaw

HAND TOOLS

Bench chisels
Clamps
Files
Handplane
Handsaw
Marking gauge
Square

MATERIALS LIST/ROUGH MILL

PART	# OF PIECES	LENGTH (IN.)	WIDTH (IN.)	THICKNESS (IN.)	WOOD	NOTES
Case Top	1	$18\frac{9}{16}$	$9\frac{1}{4}$	$\frac{11}{16}$	Primary	
Case Bottom	1	$18\frac{9}{16}$	$9\frac{1}{4}$	$\frac{11}{16}$	Primary	
Case Side	1	15	$9\frac{1}{4}$	$\frac{11}{16}$	Primary	
Case Plugs	2	12	$1\frac{1}{4}$	$1\frac{1}{4}$	Primary	
Posts	2	$11\frac{1}{16}$	$1\frac{1}{2}$	$\frac{7}{8}$	Primary	
Drawer Front	1	$17\frac{3}{8}$	$5\frac{5}{16}$	$\frac{11}{16}$	Primary	
Drawer Back	1	$17\frac{3}{8}$	5	$\frac{11}{16}$	Primary	
Drawer Sides	2	$8\frac{11}{16}$	$5\frac{5}{16}$	$\frac{11}{16}$	Primary	
Drawer Pegs	1	12	$1\frac{1}{4}$	$1\frac{1}{4}$	Primary	
Handle	1	10	$1\frac{1}{2}$	1	Primary	
Drawer Bottom	1	$16\frac{5}{8}$	$7\frac{3}{4}$	$\frac{7}{16}$	Primary	
Stiles	2	$15\frac{3}{4}$	$1\frac{3}{4}$	$\frac{7}{8}$	Primary	
Top Rail	1	$11\frac{1}{2}$	$2\frac{1}{8}$	$\frac{7}{8}$	Primary	
Bottom Rail	1	$11\frac{1}{2}$	$1\frac{3}{4}$	$\frac{7}{8}$	Primary	
Frame Peg	1	12	$1\frac{1}{4}$	$1\frac{1}{4}$	Primary	
Washer	1	8	$\frac{7}{8}$	$\frac{1}{4}$		
Case Back	1	$18\frac{1}{8}$	$6\frac{1}{16}$	$\frac{1}{2}$	Primary	
Screws	29					#4 x $\frac{3}{4}$ in.
Threaded Rod	1					12 in. with diameter to match knobs
Knobs	2					Small drawer knobs
Plywood	1	$13\frac{1}{2}$	$9\frac{1}{4}$	$\frac{1}{4}$	Cherry	For the mirror back

The rough dimensions are meant to minimize wood movement while also allowing for it. They are generally 1 in. over in length, ½ in. over in width, and ⅛ in. over in thickness. If the boards are particularly thick, wet, or warped, it may take two or more millings to get to the rough dimensions. As a rule of thumb, avoid taking more than ¼ in. of wood off of the thickness of a board in one milling.

These dimensions are based on the piece originally created; your dimensions may be different, either by design or by accident. Always check the measurements on your own project before cutting a part.

Rough milling the stock

As with any project, start by rough milling the stock. Cut out the pieces from the rough material, leaving extra length and width, then flatten one face of each piece on the jointer (**photo 1**). As you do, be aware of the grain direction in the wood and watch for tearout. If the surface starts to chip or tear, flip the board end for end so it goes over the jointer knives in the opposite direction.

Joint one face. Don't be too aggressive with the jointer. Take off no more than 1/16 in. with each pass. Make sure the jointer fence is set at 90 degrees to the bed of the jointer. After one face of the stock has been surfaced, position that face up against the fence to joint one edge (**photo 2**).

Plane to rough thickness. With the jointed face down, run the stock through the thickness planer, once again watching for tearout. Mill the boards to about 1/8 in. over their final thickness. On the tablesaw, rip boards to 1/2 in. over their final width, and cut the boards to about 1 in. over their final length.

Sticker overnight. Stack the boards with small sticks of wood, called stickers, between them and let the boards rest overnight (**photo 3**). The next day, repeat the process and bring the boards to their final thickness, width, and length. Clean up any millmarks with a handplane, then sticker overnight one more time.

Cutting Finger Joints on the Tablesaw

Very accurate finger joints can be cut on the tablesaw by using a simple technique. Start by making a cut in a piece of scrap and fitting a shim to this kerf.

Set the height of the blade so it's just shy of the layout line between the fingers, and clamp a stop block to the miter gauge so the blade cuts to the waste side of the line **(photo 1)**.

Cut the first pair of fingers in the *tops* of the side pieces, then make the corresponding cuts on the top and bottom pieces, this time inserting the shim between the stop block and the workpiece. The shim will move the board over the width of the sawblade so the kerf is on the opposite side of the layout line **(photo 2)**.

Reset the stop block for the second set of fingers on the top of the side pieces, make those cuts, and repeat the sequence with the shim for the top and bottom pieces.

The *bottoms* of the side pieces are cut the same way, but the fingers are longer. The two outer fingers become legs for the case; the middle fingers are trimmed back. The height of the blade should be adjusted so it falls just below the layout line.

Remove the waste between the cuts on a bandsaw **(photo 3)**, then pare to the layout line with a chisel **(photo 4)**.

T-Mac Tip

When using the bandsaw, make sure the blade is very tight and the guard is just above the workpiece.

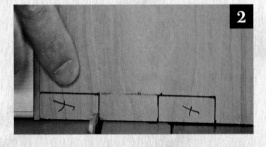

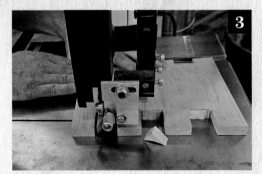

Laying out the joints

The case and drawer are formed by inter-locking fingers that fit together tightly. There are a lot of fingers to cut, and this would be slow and difficult work done by hand. To speed up the process and make it more accurate, make the cuts on a tablesaw following the technique in Build Your Skills on the facing page.

Lay out the finger locations on the case pieces. Start by taking two adjoining pieces and laying them on the bench end to end. Using a marking gauge or a combination square set to 1¼ in., mark the width of the first finger on the edge of one of the pieces (**photo 1**). Without changing the setting, mark the other side of the board (**photo 2**). Then mark the other piece (**photo 3**). To ensure there will be no mistakes about the location of the fingers, mark both sides of the board and also across the end grain.

Reset the marking gauge to 2½ in. and repeat the process to lay out the location of the second set of fingers, and then again at 3¾ in. to complete the layout. When you're finished, the location of all the fingers will be clearly marked (**photo 4**). Using the shim and the technique described in Build Your Skills, the tablesaw blade will make a cut on opposite sides of each common layout line (**photo 5**). This ensures a perfect fit.

T-Mac Tip

We're using a black felt-tip pen to draw the layout lines so they show up clearly in the photos. But the ink can bleed into the wood fibers and be difficult to remove later. When you're doing this work in the shop, use a marking gauge or a pencil instead.

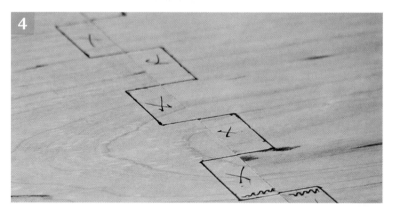

Visiting the Gamble House

There's no better place to learn about the work of Charles and Henry Greene than the Gamble House in Pasadena, California. Designed in 1908 for Mary and David Gamble, the house has been called the ultimate expression of the Arts and Crafts movement.

One of the remarkable things about the house is how it unifies architecture and furniture. Both the house and its furnishings have similar detailing, including the softly rounded corners and ebony plugs that have become signature features of the Greene and Greene style.

As Gamble House director Edward "Ted" Bosley explains, not only was each piece of furniture designed for a specific room in the house, but it was also intended for a specific location in the room.

Greene and Greene designs often incorporated stained glass, such as the light fixtures that are featured prominently throughout the house. The Greenes also

The Gamble House.

used inlays of silver or exotic hardwoods in furniture.

The guest bedroom contains some of the most beautiful furnishings in the house, including a dressing mirror with a pivoting mirror frame and drawers complete with silver drawer pulls. The Gambles believed that the finest furniture should be enjoyed by their house guests, so that's where their best furniture could be found.

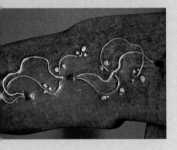

Hallmarks of Greene and Greene designs: softly rounded corners and pegged connections (top); stained glass light fixtures (center); delicate silver inlays (bottom).

Left: A dressing mirror with a pivoting mirror frame and three drawers.

Above: Silver drawer pulls on the dressing mirror.

Rabbeting the Case

Mark the rabbet locations. Once all of the joints have been pared, dry-fit the case and clamp it together. Mark the back of the case for the ⅜-in. by ⅜-in. rabbet that will hold the back boards (**photo 1**). While the case is clamped together, make the feet by marking out the inner fingers at the bottom of the side pieces (**photo 2**). To create the "pillowed" look on the ends of the fingers, leave the fingers 1/32 in. long, then make the cuts on the bandsaw (**photo 3**).

Rabbets are cut on a router table. On the top and bottom pieces, the rabbet can be run the full length of the board. But on the side pieces, the rabbet must be stopped short of the end.

Set the router table fence. If you're using a split fence on the router table, set it so each side just misses the router bit (**photo 4**). This will make it clear where the cut starts and stops. Then set a stop block so the side pieces can be tipped safely into the bit (**photo 5**). Remember that the block will have to be adjusted to cut the right- and left-hand pieces (**photo 6**).

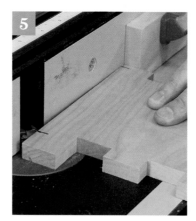

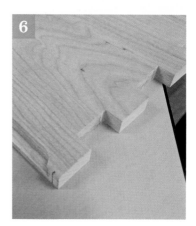

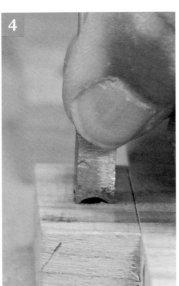

Assembling the case

Drill holes for the plugs. The ebony plugs at each joint are a nice detail in this project. Adding them is a three-part process. First, make a ³⁄₈-in.-deep hole big enough for the head of the screw at each joint. These holes are ³⁄₁₆ in., centered in the width of each finger (**photo 1**).

Drill root holes. Second, assemble the case, check it for square, and drill root holes through the center of each plug hole into the end grain of the other piece (**photo 2**). The diameter should be slightly less than the threaded diameter of the screw. Take the case apart and drill out the pilot holes at the bottom of each plug hole. The holes should be large enough so the screw threads don't catch.

Square the holes to accept the plugs. Make a squaring tool by filing a piece of steel to a ³⁄₁₆-in. square and hollowing the tip with a round file so the corners come to points (**photo 3**). Tap the end of the tool with a hammer to turn the round hole into a square hole (**photo 4**). If the punch doesn't go deep enough, continue with a small chisel. Be careful when hammering the squaring tool—striking too hard can split the board ends.

Add post mortises. With the case disassembled, lay out the twin mortises for the mirror posts in the top piece and cut them with either a mortising machine or a drill and chisel (**photo 5**).

T-Mac Tip

Lay out and cut a mortise like the one in the top on a piece of scrap. Fit the tenons to the scrap rather than the finished top to avoid damaging the top of the case in the process.

Gluing up the case. To lessen the stress surrounding the gluing up of the box, approach it one side at a time. Dry-clamp the bottom of the case together, apply glue to the fingers on the top and side pieces (**photo 6**), then assemble and clamp the whole box together. After checking it for square, secure the corners together using screws (**photo 7**). Then glue and screw the bottom of the case together.

Pillow the fingers. The fingers have been left a little long intentionally so they can be rounded over to create the pillowed effect. It's done with a chisel and then a block wrapped in sandpaper (**photo 8**).

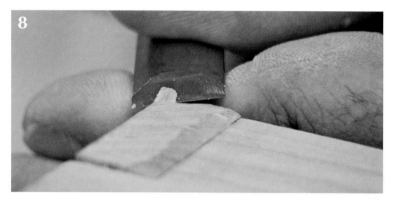

Cut material for the plugs. Rip lengths of plug material, cut them to length with a fine-tooth handsaw, and chamfer one end of each plug. Next, dip the plugs in glue and tap them into the square holes. Use a piece of veneer, as shown (**photo 9**), so the plug isn't driven flush with the surface, and then pillow the end of each plug with a chisel.

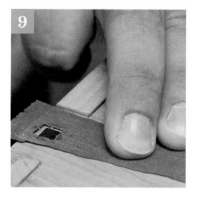

Cut the mirror posts. Once all of the plugs have been inserted and all of the fingers and plugs pillowed, cut two mirror posts and tenons on one end of each until they fit snugly into the twin mortises in the top of the case (**photo 10**). To do this, cut a ⁹⁄₁₆-in. by ⅛-in. rabbet all the way around the bottom of the posts, then mark the section in the middle that must be removed. The twin tenons are created by cutting away the waste on the tablesaw (**photo 11**). The posts can be left square, or tapered slightly, whichever you prefer.

Making the mirror frame

The frame for the mirror is assembled with slip joints. The two side pieces are identical, and the top and bottom are the same length and thickness but slightly different widths. The top piece has to be slightly wider to allow for the cloud lift detail (**photo 1**).

Cut out the cloud lift. Lay out the cloud lift as shown in the drawings on pp. 4–5, cut the profile on the bandsaw (**photo 2**), and then use files, chisels, and gouges—whatever it takes—to smooth all the edges. Glue up the frame; use clamps running the length and width of the frame, plus hand screws to clamp each corner together. Then mark the location of two ebony plugs on a diagonal at each corner, drill and square the holes, and glue in the plugs.

Cut rabbets for the mirror and back. The back of the frame has two rabbets cut to two different depths, one for the mirror and one for the back (**photo 3**). They are cut with a top-bearing router bit and a shopmade jig to guide it (**photo 4**).

Add frame pivots. The frame pivots on a length of threaded rod that is bent at one end and set into a shallow recess in the back of the frame (**photo 5**). Drill the hole for the pivot midway up the length of the frame, 7½ in., and up 8½ in. from the shoulder of the post where it meets the case.

Once the holes for the pivot have been drilled in the posts, glue the posts into the case.

Adding the drawer

You don't have to make a drawer. The recess in the front of the case could also be filled with a decorative panel, but adding the drawer makes the project more useful (**photo 1**).

Make the drawer. The drawer is made just like the case, with finger joints that are glued, screwed, and plugged with ebony. The drawer bottom is set in a groove cut on the inside faces of the drawer parts. On the front corners, cut a rabbet into the side pieces so the groove won't be visible on the front of the drawer (**photo 2**).

One difference between the drawer and the case is that the fingers are flush, without pillowing, so the drawer fits the opening precisely. On the back piece of the drawer, cut away the material from the top of the groove down so the drawer bottom can slide in from the back. Anchor the bottom with a single screw that runs up through the drawer bottom into the back piece.

Make the drawer handle. Like the mirror frame, the drawer handle has a cloud-lift motif. Cut it out and smooth the edges just as you did with the top of the mirror frame.

Finishing the piece

All that's left is the finish. For this project, I applied one thin coat of tung oil and then sprayed on multiple coats of nitrocellulose lacquer, sanding between coats with 320-grit paper. Whatever finish you choose, just be sure to follow the manufacturer's instructions when applying it.

ARTS AND CRAFTS ARMCHAIR

Laying Out and Cutting Curved Parts

Craftsmen have been making chairs since before the time of the Egyptians, and they have been created in many different styles and materials. This classic armchair is inspired by Arts and Crafts designs, and it makes a great intermediate wood-working project.

The parts are relatively simple: four legs, stretchers, a back with curved slats, curved arms, and upholstered cushions for the seat and the back. The angle of the back can be adjusted for various sitting positions. The side stretchers slope downward slightly from front to back, putting the seat at a comfortable angle. Although that complicates construction somewhat, it's well worth the effort.

Through-tenons at the top of the legs pop right through the arms, creating a great visual detail. The arm also slopes downward from front to back, giving the chair graceful lines.

Laying out and cutting the various curved parts is one of the challenges of this project, but it's easier than you'd imagine. All it takes is basic shop tools and a jig for the router table.

The species of wood is another key part of the design. Although you could make this from cherry, walnut, or another hardwood, white oak is a traditional choice for this style chair, and that's what we selected. To add even more dimension to the wood, we fumed the chair with ammonia, enhancing its figure and color.

Armchair

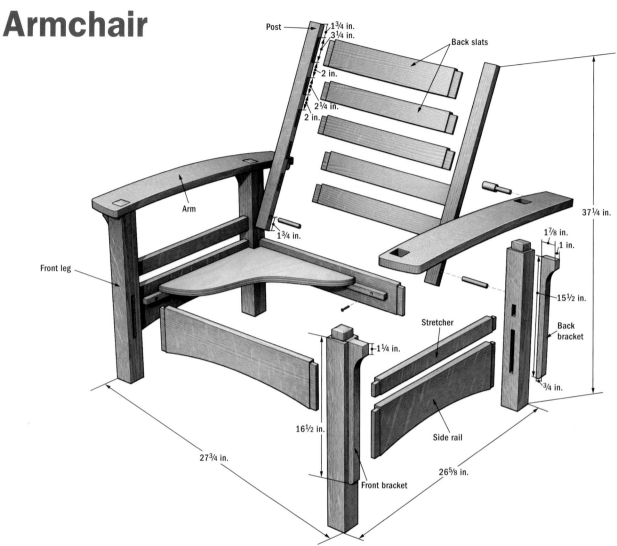

Post

1¾ in.
3¼ in.
2 in.
2¼ in.
2 in.

Back slats

Arm

1¾ in.

37¼ in.

1⅞ in.
1 in.

15½ in.

Back bracket

¾ in.

Front leg

Stretcher

1¼ in.

Side rail

16½ in.

Front bracket

27¾ in.

26⅝ in.

Corner Detail

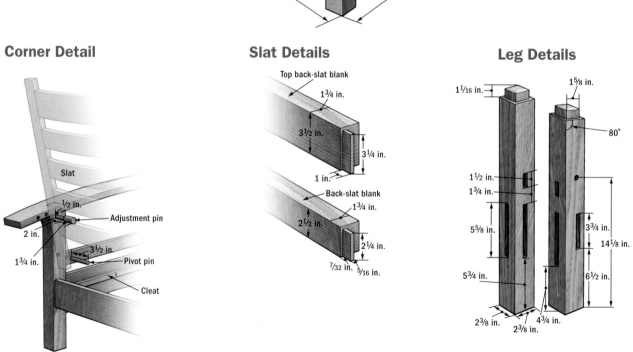

Slat

½ in.
2 in.
1¾ in.
3½ in.

Adjustment pin

Pivot pin

Cleat

Slat Details

Top back-slat blank

1¾ in.

3½ in.
3¼ in.

1 in.

Back-slat blank

1¾ in.

2½ in.
2¼ in.

7/32
5/16 in.

Leg Details

1 1/16 in.

1⅝ in.

80°

1½ in.
1¾ in.

5⅝ in.

3¾ in.
14⅛ in.

5¾ in.

6½ in.

2⅜ in.
2⅜ in.
4¾ in.

MATERIALS LIST/ROUGH MILL

PART	# OF PIECES	LENGTH (IN.)	WIDTH (IN.)	THICKNESS (IN.)	WOOD
Front Legs	2	24¼	2½	2½	Primary
Back Legs	2	22¹⁵⁄₃₂	2½	2½	Primary
Front Brackets	2	17½	2⅜	1⅛	Primary
Back Brackets	2	16½	2⅜	1⅛	Primary
Front Rail	1	25¾	6⅜	1	Primary
Back Rail	1	25¾	4½	1	Primary
Side Rails	2	24⅞	6⅜	1	Primary
Stretchers	2	24¾	2¼	1	Primary
Posts	2	28¼	2¼	1	Primary
Top Back Slat	1	22	4	1⅞	Primary
Back Slats	4	22	3	1⅞	Primary
Arms	2	35	5½	2	Primary
Cleats	4	21	1	1	Primary
Pivot Pin	1	12	¾	¾	Primary
Adjustment Pin	1	12	1	1	Primary
Plywood Seat	1	24¼	23¾	¾	
Cushions	2	22	23	5	
Plywood (for jig)	1	25	3	¾	

The first step of any project is to turn the rough material into parts at their finished dimensions. This is a two-part process carried out over two days. It's explained in more detail on p. 7.

on p. 7.

TOOL LIST

POWER TOOLS
Bandsaw
Cordless drill
Drill press
Jointer
Mortising machine
Router table
Sander
Tablesaw
Thickness planer

HAND TOOLS
Bench chisels
Bench planes
Combination
  square
Flexible steel ruler
Marking gauge
Spokeshave

Arm Profile

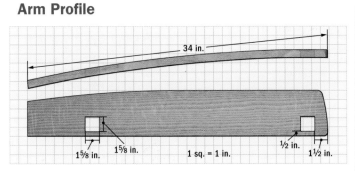

34 in.

1⅝ in.   1⅝ in.   1 sq. = 1 in.   ½ in.   1½ in.

Stretcher and Bracket

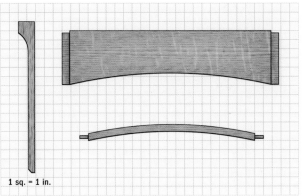

1 sq. = 1 in.

Making the legs

Once the stock for the legs has been finished to $2\frac{3}{8}$ in. square and the legs cut to their finished lengths, the tops of the back legs must be cut at an angle so they fit the downward sweep of the arm. Set an adjustable bevel to 10 degrees (**photo 1**), mark the tops of both back legs (**photo 2**), and make the cuts on a chopsaw (**photo 3**).

Lay out the mortises. To lay out all the mortises for the rails and stretchers, set a combination square to the distance between the bottom of the front leg and the bottom of the mortise for the side rail and mark the leg at that location. Then continue the square line across the face of the leg (**photo 4**). Use a longer combination square to mark the top of the mortise, indexing both layout marks from the bottom of the leg (**photo 5**).

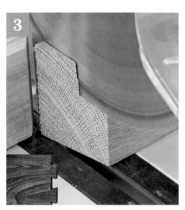

Cut the mortises. When the length of the mortise has been marked on the leg, use a marking gauge to mark the width (**photo 6**). Then cut the mortise with a mortising machine, making sure you set the depth adjustment and fence correctly (**photo 7**).

Continue laying out and cutting the mortises on all four legs. All of the mortises are $1/2$ in. wide and $7/8$ in. deep. Check the drawing on p. 18 for their correct locations.

After cleaning up the inside faces of the mortises with a sharp chisel (**photo 8**), mark the location of the hole for the back rest pivot on the inside face of each back leg and bore the holes on a drill press (**photo 9**).

Tenon the legs. The last step is to cut the tenons on the tops of the legs. Start by setting a marking gauge about $3/16$ in. more than the thickness of the arm and scribing all the way around the top of each leg (**photo 10**). Using a second marking gauge set at $3/8$ in., scribe the ends of all the tops to define the cheek cuts (**photo 11**), and then use a dado blade on the tablesaw to remove the waste.

Remember, the miter gauge will be set at 90 degrees for the front legs, but because the back legs are cut at an angle, the miter gauge will have to be set to a matching angle of 10 degrees. Cut one side of the leg, flip the leg over, and readjust the miter gauge to 10 degrees in the opposite direction and make the second pass (**photo 12**).

Because of the angled top, the remaining waste (on the front and back faces of the leg) will have to be removed with a bandsaw or by hand. Clean up the cuts to the scribed lines with a chisel.

Making stretchers and rails

Both ends of the front rails are cut at 90 degrees. But the side rails and stretchers are cut at 2½ degrees to pitch the seat back and make the chair more comfortable.

Cut the side rail tenons. To cut the tenons on the side rails and stretchers, set a marking gauge to ⅞ in., the length of the tenon, and scribe a line around the ends of one of the pieces. At the tablesaw, set the miter gauge to 2½ degrees.

If the dado blade is still set at ¹⁵⁄₁₆ in. from when you cut the tenons for the legs, you can either change out the blades or you'll need to attach a scrap piece of wood to make a sacrificial fence. The idea behind the sacrificial fence is that you can adjust the width, in this case to ⅞ in., and raise the dado blade up through the sacrificial fence until it reaches the proper height. Doing this will protect your primary fence (**photo 1**).

Set the blade height to ⅛ in., align the blade with the scribe mark, and cut all the outside faces of the rails and stretchers

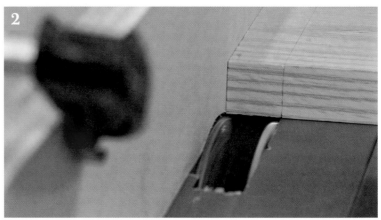

(photo 2). Next, flip the boards over, raise the blade, and make tests cuts on the back side until the tenons fit into the mortises. The depth of cut will be about ¼ in. Remember that because of the angle you'll have to readjust the miter gauge to make half of these cuts.

All of the tenons get a ¼-in. shoulder on the top. In addition, trim the bottom edge of the back tenons on the side rails and stretchers so they're perpendicular to the ends of the boards. This is easily achieved by working with a chisel at the bench (photo 3).

Add the curves. One of the design elements is a curve in the bottom of the side and front rails, which lightens the overall look of the chair. The curves are easy to lay out with the help of a flexible ruler (photo 4). Find the center of the rail, mark the highest point of the arc, and flex the ruler to meet this point. Having a second set of hands is a big help.

Make the cuts on a bandsaw and clean them up with a spokeshave (photo 5) and sandpaper.

T-Mac Tip

When laying out tenons with a marking gauge, you can scribe the ends of all the pieces if you want. But you can also mark just one end and use those scribe lines to set up the tablesaw. Once the saw is set, it's not going to change, so you don't really need scribe lines on any other pieces.

Once all of the stretchers and legs have been cleaned and properly fitted to the mortises, it's time to glue up the sides of the chair.

Sam Maloof: A Visionary

Top and bottom: Sam Maloof's most enduring design–his graceful rocking chair.

Sam Maloof may be best remembered for his rocking chairs, but a visit to his home in Alta Loma, California, and a tour with his wife, Beverley, proves that his artistic talents and interests were much broader.

The original living space in what became the Maloof compound was only 400 sq. ft., and was packed with the furniture that Sam designed and built, as well as other artwork that captured his interest.

As Harold Nelson, curator of American Decorative Arts at Huntington, put it, Sam was the "quintessential designer-craftsman."

You have only to see the many pieces he designed, including a beautiful spiral staircase (shown at right), to understand how much he influenced American craft.

The highlight of this *Rough Cut* Road Trip was showing on camera the beauty and smoothness of what was commonly referred to as "the California curve."

Maloof's work went well beyond furniture to include architectural features like this spiral stair.

Maloof also collected pieces by other artisans that he admired.

Making the back

One of the nice features of this chair is the adjustable back, which consists of two posts and five curved slats. The back pivots on a $1/2$-in.-diameter pin.

Mortise the posts. The posts are $7/8$ in. thick and $1^3/4$ in. wide. They're mortised along their length for the slat tenons (**photo 1**). Mortises are $5/16$ in. wide, 1 in. deep, and centered on the posts. For the mortise locations, check the drawing on p. 18. Mortises for the crest rail are slightly longer than those for the other four slats.

After cutting all of the mortises, bore the hole for the pivot at the bottom of each post (**photo 2**). The hole is drilled $1^3/4$ in. up from the bottom of the post, drilled all the way through.

Tenon the slats. The curved slats start with stock that's $1^3/4$ in thick. Scribe the tenon locations with a marking gauge and remove the waste with a dado blade on the tablesaw. Cut the shoulder on the inside face at $7/32$ in. (**photo 3**), then remove the waste on the outside face so the tenons fit the mortises (they'll still need to be haunched).

Shaping Curved Parts

You can make curved furniture components by roughing them out on a bandsaw and then refining the shape with hand and power tools. The trick is making the parts uniform. Here's how we did that with these slats.

At this point, the slats are still rectangular. To bring them to their finished shape, I start by making a jig **(photo 1)**. The base is a piece of plywood cut to the curve. Two end blocks can be made on the tablesaw and will hold the tenons.

With the slat in the jig, the curves can be traced on one edge **(photo 2)**. Take the slat out of the jig and cut it to rough shape on the bandsaw **(photo 3)**.

To finish the part, put the slat back in the jig and run it over a top-bearing bit on the router table **(photo 4)**. With so much bit exposed, this is potentially a dangerous procedure, so be very careful to keep your hands clear and wear ear and eye protection as well as a dust mask.

Run the slat over the bit on both sides of the jig, flip the slat over, and make two more passes. The slats will still need to be cleaned up, but most of the work is done and the shapes will all be the same.

To remove the millmarks, you can use a sander, spokeshave, or whatever tool works best. When the slats are finished, glue up the back **(photo 5)**.

1

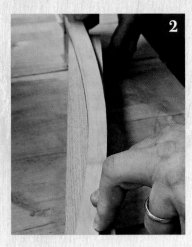

2

3

4

5

Making the arms

Draw the curves. The arms start as blanks 5 in. wide, 1⅞ in. thick, and 34 in. long. Find the midpoint of the arm, measure up 1 in. from the bottom edge, and then bend your ruler so it intersects the top mark and the two corners (**photo 1**). Draw the curved line, and then make the cut on the bandsaw (**photo 2**).

Clean up the cuts. Clean up the millmarks on the inside of the curve with a spokeshave or tool of your choice (**photo 3**). Then, using a square, marking gauge, or just your finger as a guide, mark off the top of the arm so it follows the curved side that you've just finished (**photo 4**). Cut out the curve on the bandsaw and clean up the sawmarks.

Mark the mortise locations. Now it's time to mark the location of the mortises in the top of the arm to correspond with the tenons on the tops of the legs. Rest the arm on the shoulder cuts of the posts with 1½ in. overhanging the front and mark the locations for the tenons on the edge of the arm (**photo 5**). Then lay out the inside edge of the mortise ½ in. from the edge (**photo 6**).

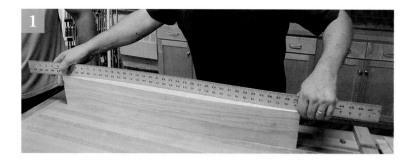

Cut the mortises. Cut the mortises all the way through the arm, using the scribed lines on the edge of the arm as a guide for getting the right angle. Drill out most of the waste and finish up with a chisel, chopping out the waste from both sides.

Fit the arm. Now the arm can be fitted over the tenons (**photo 7**). With the arm in place, mark the tenons where they meet the top surface (**photo 8**). These marks will be your guide for beveling the tenons where they come through. Beveling is done with a chisel.

Shape the arm. To give the arm a more graceful look, lay out the curves on the front and the curved taper along the outside edge. Then carefully make the cuts at the bandsaw. Once the curves are cut, clean them up with a handplane and sandpaper and break all of the edges.

Glue up the chair. The rest of the chair can now be glued, with the exception of the arms. To attach the back, wax one end of the pivot pins and run the waxed ends through the posts and into the holes in the back legs. Apply glue to the trailing ends of the pins before driving them all the way into the posts. The back will pivot on the pins and come to rest on dowels fitted into the back of the arms (**photo 9**).

Finishing up

Add cleats for the seat. You'll need to attach cleats to the inside edge of each rail, 1½ in. down from the top edge, to support the seat. Once they're in, cut a piece of ¾-in. plywood to fit, notching the corners around the legs **(photos 1 and 2).**

Set pin locations. To set the adjustment pins, you'll first need to find a comfortable location for the back. By using a clamp as a stop, you can fiddle with the position until you find something you like. You're then ready to lay out and drill ½-in.-dia. holes 2 in. deep at each location. The pins are 4 in. long, with the first 2 in. cut to ½ in. dia. to fit the holes. The knobs of the pins are ⅞ in.

Now the arms can be glued in place and the brackets cut out and glued to the outside faces of the legs.

Sand and finish. When all glue residue has been removed, and all surfaces sanded smooth, apply the finish of your choice following the manufacturer's instructions.

For this chair we used lacquer as the final finish, but before applying we made a tent for the chair and placed a bowl of household ammonia inside, a process known as fuming. The ammonia vapor colors the wood and gives it a beautiful tone. Be careful—this process can be dangerous. Make sure you read up on it before trying it, and take all appropriate safety precautions.

PIE CRUST TRAY

Learning to Carve with the Grain

This mahogany pie crust tray has a lot in common with the tilting tables that were used in colonial New England. The characteristic detail is the serpentine pattern around the perimeter that combines bead and cove shapes carved by hand.

Although it looks complex in its finished form, the pie crust edge is less challenging than it appears. It begins with a fairly simple plywood pattern that is traced around the perimeter of a turned blank. Step by step, the edge is brought to its final shape using a bandsaw, a few hand tools including files and rasps, carving chisels, a router plane, and a heavy dose of patience.

Much of the work of this project involves carving by hand and learning how to read the grain of wood. Because wood can easily chip or tear, you need to approach it from the right direction to ensure a clean, chip-free profile. Paying attention to how the wood is reacting to the edge of the tool is the name of the game. Remember that a very sharp tool is your best friend.

This project requires very little in the way of materials—just 1 bd. ft. that will probably cost you less than $20, along with a few scraps of plywood.

Our tray is made from mahogany, which is not only a traditional choice but also a practical one because it carves cleanly. If you are a beginner, look for a piece without too much wild grain, which can be challenging to carve. However, a more advanced carver might consider using a gnarly wood that will give you a more dramatic look.

Pie Crust Tray

Bead

12 in.

Cove

15/16 in.

Pie Crust Profile

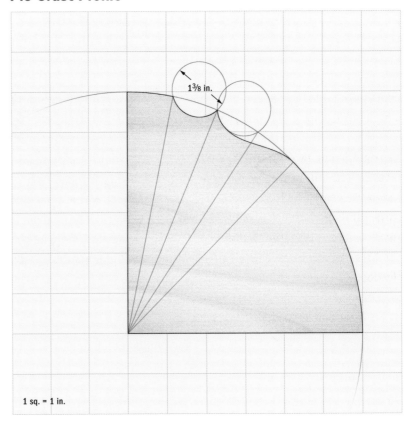

1 3/8 in.

1 sq. = 1 in.

MATERIALS LIST/ROUGH MILL

PART	# OF PIECES	LENGTH (IN.)	WIDTH (IN.)	THICKNESS (IN.)	WOOD	NOTES
Tray	1	13	12½	1	Primary	
Kraft Paper	1					8-in.-dia. piece
Plywood	1					8-in. round, ¾ in. thick
Screws	6					¾ in. long

The rough dimensions are meant to minimize wood movement while also allowing for it. They are generally 1 in. over in length, ½ in. over in width, and ⅛ in. over in thickness. If the boards are particularly thick, wet, or warped, it may take two or more millings to get to the rough dimensions. As a rule of thumb, avoid taking more than ¼ in. of wood off of the thickness of a board in one milling.

These dimensions are based on the piece originally created; your dimensions may be different, either by design or by accident. Always check the measurements on your own project before cutting a part.

TOOL LIST

POWER TOOLS
Bandsaw
Lathe
Sander

HAND TOOLS
Bench chisels
Bench plane
Carving chisels
File
Rasp
Router plane

Serpentine Edge

Profile Detail

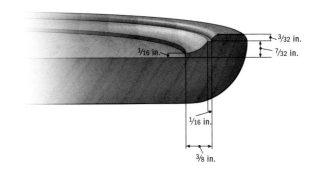

Cutting out the blank

Start with a piece of wood 12 in. or 12½ in. square and 1 in. thick. The blank doesn't need the usual rough and finish milling procedure because most of the initial work is done on a lathe. All you really need to do is flatten one face with a handplane (**photo 1**).

Turning a Perfect Circle

This serving tray starts with a perfectly round blank, and the easiest way to get it is by turning it on the lathe. We don't want anything to mar the bottom of the tray when we're done, so the challenge is to mount the blank on the lathe face plate without leaving screw holes in the bottom.

The answer is to glue an intermediate layer of plywood to the bottom of the blank, do the turning, and then remove the plywood. Here's how to do it.

On a piece of void-free ¾-in. plywood, use a compass to draw a circle with a diameter of 8 in. **(photo 1),** then draw a second circle from the same center point that's about the same size as the face plate for the lathe **(photo 2).** At the bandsaw, cut the plywood to the outer circle **(photo 3).**

On the back of the blank, find the center point and from it draw a 12-in. circle with a compass. From the same point, draw an 8-in. circle on the plywood.

Glue the plywood to the blank with a piece of brown kraft paper between the two **(photo 4).** Don't use too much clamping pressure. Allow the glue to dry overnight, then cut the tray blank to the outside of the 12-in.-dia. line.

When the glue has dried, the plywood can be popped off, as shown on p. 39, and any residual kraft paper removed with a handplane.

Making the pattern

The pie crust profile on the edge of the tray is laid out with a pattern made from ¼-in. plywood (**photo 1**). The pattern is one-quarter the size of the tray, but the repeating serpentine design is cut on one-half of the pattern, or one-eighth of the circumference of the tray. The tray is marked one quadrant at a time by tracing the profile, flipping the pattern over, and tracing it a second time. This keeps the design symmetrical as you work your way around the tray.

Lay out the shapes. On a piece of ¼-in. plywood, draw the finished size of the pattern so it will be exactly one-quarter the size of the tray. Then bisect the arc with a straightedge (**photo 2**). Divide one side of the pattern into quarters, and lay out the curves so they look like the drawing on p. 32. Cut the pattern to shape on the bandsaw and smooth the edges with a file or sandpaper (**photo 3**).

Tea Time at the Museum of Fine Arts

This tray is patterned after the tilting tea tables and silver tea services of the 18th century, both of which are on display at the Museum of Fine Arts in Boston.

Some of Paul Revere's finest work is in this collection, including a beautifully decorated rococo-style silver tray with elegant cabriole legs.

This silver tray would have been used to hold a tea service on a special kind of table. Once the tea was served, the tabletop could be rotated to deliver the hot tea to a seated guest without anyone having to get up.

More elaborate tea tables, like the Philadelphia tilt-top shown below, incorporated a carved serpentine edge. The process used in making this 18th-century table is similar to the one used in making our tray.

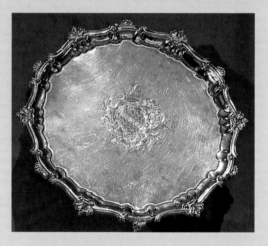

Some of Paul Revere's best work can be found at the Museum of Fine Arts in Boston.

This Philadelphia tilt-top table has a carved edge very much like the serving tray.

An elaborate silver tea service with a sculpted edge would have been used on a table with a rotating top.

Turning the blank

Once the glue has dried overnight, screw the faceplate to the plywood with #8 by 1-in. screws and mount the blank on the lathe **(photo 1).** Use the tool rest and a pencil to mark the edge at the largest diameter that can be obtained from the blank **(photo 2).** Remove the blank from the lathe, and cut just to the outside of the line on the bandsaw or with a jigsaw to make the blank roughly circular.

Size the blank. Put the blank back on the lathe and turn the outside edge to make a perfect circle **(photo 3).** Then, flatten the back face of the blank from the edge inward by 2 in. to 3 in., taking off a very small amount of material as you go.

True the face. Flatten the face of the blank and bring it to its final thickness of $^{15}/_{16}$ in. **(photo 4).** Check your work with a straightedge to make sure it's flat **(photo 5).**

T-Mac Tip

Make all the cuts on the lathe with scraping tools, taking light cuts. It's not a race. Take your time and work up to your lines slowly.

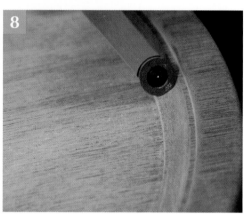

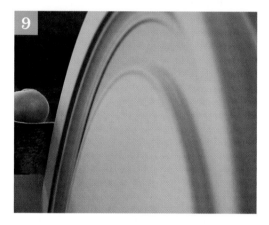

Add the bead and cove. Refer to the drawing on p. 33. First, lay out the $9/16$-in. bead and then the $3/8$-in. cove on the edge of the blank using a pencil and the tool rest **(photo 6)**. The third line a few inches inside of the cove defines an area where material will be removed to a depth of $5/16$. This sets the depth of the tray and also gives your tools room to work as you cut the bead and the cove.

Make the cuts. Slowly work the area inside of the innermost layout line, taking out material until the area is $5/16$ in. deep **(photo 7)**. Check the depth, and when it's correct, shape the bead and the cove by marking and cutting the flats as indicated on the drawing and then connecting them with the cove **(photo 8)**.

Finish the bead. Round over the inside and outside edges of the bead and add the curve on the outside edge of the blank. Sand the turned areas while the blank is still on the lathe **(photo 9)**. Then turn the interior of the tray, periodically stopping the lathe and checking the surface with a straightedge. Once the interior surface of the tray is flat, you can clean up with a piece of 150- or 220-grit sandpaper.

Making the serpentine edge

Remove the faceplate. Back at the bench, mount the blank in a vise and, using a couple of wide bench chisels, pop the plywood off **(photo 1).** Note: Be aware of grain direction and make sure you're going with the grain, not against it. If you go against the grain, you could end up breaking the tray.

To get started, tap the first chisel in to create a void, then use a second chisel to continue widening the gap. Work your way around the piece of plywood until the two boards separate, being careful not to dig the chisel into the back of the tray. Remember to clean the remaining paper and glue off the back of the tray using a bench plane, sander, or your tool of choice.

Transfer the pattern. Check to make sure the pattern is one-quarter of the circumference of the tray. If your tray is a little smaller or larger than 12 in. don't worry. What's nice about this design is that you have flexibility.

If the pattern is off—that is, if it doesn't walk around the tray in four equal steps—you'll have to make any adjustments in the flats by making them longer or shorter. Mark the edge where the pattern will start, align the pattern and trace the serpentine edge on the first quadrant, flip the pattern over, and mark the other side of the quadrant **(photo 2).** Repeat the process all the way around the tray, quadrant by quadrant. Try to align the points of the quarter pattern, making sure that it sits 90 degrees to the grain.

Remove the waste. At the bandsaw, remove the waste outside the

layout lines. Be careful not to damage the points of the profile **(photo 3).**

File the profile smooth. With a half-round file, clean up the bandsaw marks **(photo 4).**

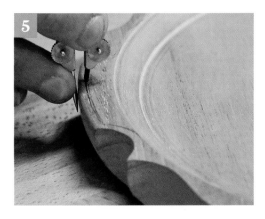

Trace the bead. Using a compass with one leg left long to act as a fence, trace the 3/16-in.-wide bead along the edge of the tray (**photo 5**).

Chop the bead. Clamp the tray to the bench and use gouges to chop the inner edge of the bead with a series of downward stabbing cuts (**photo 6**).

Remove the waste. Use a gouge to rough out the shape of the bead. Make light cuts and pay careful attention to the grain of the wood to avoid tearout (**photo 7**). As you work around the perimeter of the tray, you'll have to change your approach depending on the direction of the grain.

Finish up with a router plane. Cut a spacer block to the same depth as the moldings. Use a router plane riding on the molding and the spacer block to

establish the depth of the fillet **(photo 8).** Work your way around the tray until it looks like the one in **photo 9.**

Shape the cove. Set the compass to the outside edge of the cove—about $9/16$ in. You'll then use it to lay out the shape of the cove **(photo 10)** just as you did with the bead. Work your way around the perimeter, then use gouges to chop out the shape **(photo 11).** Be extremely careful not to make the chopping cuts too deep. Then remove the waste with a gouge and router plane.

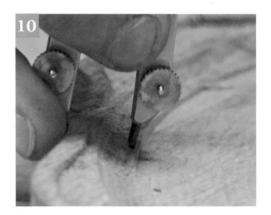

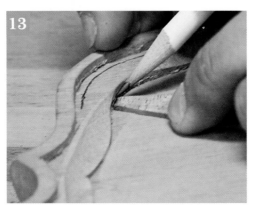

Lay out the molding. Using a spacer block that's ¹⁄₁₆ in. thick, trace the molding along the edge of the tray (**photo 12**). Use the same spacer block to draw a second line to establish the depth (**photo 13**).

T-Mac Tip

To make the crisp transition lines between sections of the cove, roll the gouge out of the cut as you approach a crest to avoid cutting the bottom corner too deeply.

Connect the lines. With a gouge and a back-bent gouge, carve away the material between the two lines you've just drawn for both the bead and cove (**photo 14**). Be mindful of the grain direction. Once the entire molding is carved, clean and smooth both inside and out using 220-grit sandpaper.

Round over the back. Using a rasp, then a file, and finally sandpaper, round over the back edge of the tray (**photo 15**).

Adding the finish

To finish the tray, I start with a thin coat of boiled linseed oil, which really brings out the color and figure of the wood (**photo 1**).

After the oil has dried, add several coats of shellac. With a project this small, an aerosol can works fine.

You can buff out the finish with 4/0 steel wool before you add the final coat of shellac. When the last coat has dried, add a layer of dark wax. You'll see 200 years of patina develop in an instant (**photo 2**).

SERVING CART

Culling the Best Material from Oversize Stock

This rolling cart is perfect for serving coffee and dessert or as a mobile work surface for dinner parties. The base is constructed out of tiger maple, and the top is a durable, man-made quartz composite.

There are two shelves made from $9/16$-in.-thick slats that can be placed wherever they will work best for you. This design is also completely flexible, so the cart can be built to suit any space.

A nice feature of the cart is that it is mobile, thanks to two simple shop-made plywood wheels. What makes the design of this project pop, though, is the careful use and placement of

highly figured tiger maple. To maximize the figured maple, start with a 2-in. flatsawn board, and cut and mill it into quartersawn pieces. Select highly figured pieces for the most visible parts of the cart. The best figured pieces should be on the front. You should also feel free to experiment with grain direction. Different patterns can be created by simply changing the orientation of the pieces.

What's great is that the entire cart can be assembled with simple mortise-and-tenon construction and the use of some standard shop tools. The top is attached with a bead of silicone.

Serving Cart

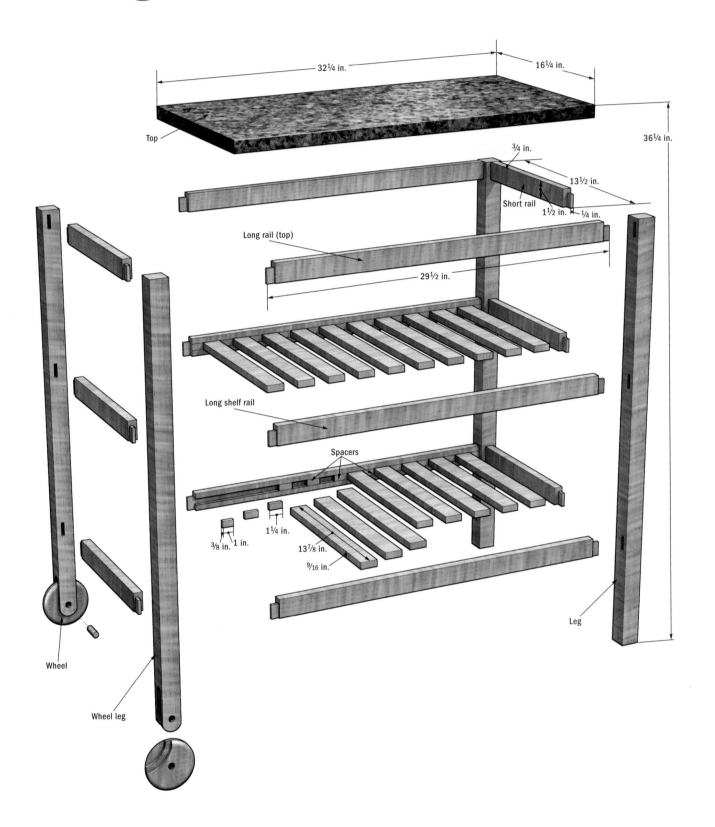

32¼ in.

16¼ in.

Top

¾ in.

13½ in.

36¼ in.

Short rail

1½ in.   ¼ in.

Long rail (top)

29½ in.

Long shelf rail

Spacers

1¼ in.

⅜ in.   1 in.

13⅞ in.

⁹⁄₁₆ in.

Leg

Wheel

Wheel leg

MATERIALS LIST/ROUGH MILL

PART	# OF PIECES	LENGTH (IN.)	WIDTH (IN.)	THICKNESS (IN.)	WOOD	NOTES
Legs	4	36	1⅝	1⅝	Primary	
Long Rail	6	36	1⅝	⅞	Primary	
Short Rail	3	36	1⅝	⅞	Primary	
Slats	10	36	1⅝	¾	Primary	
Spacers	11	18	1⅝	¾	Primary	
Wheels	2	15	5	⅜	Plywood	
Dowels	2					½ in. diameter x 1½ in.
Top	1					16¼ in. x 32¼ in.

TOOL LIST

POWER TOOLS
Jointer
Mortising machine
Tablesaw
Thickness planer

HAND TOOLS
Bench plane
Combination square
Fine-tooth saw
Shoulder plane

Cart connections

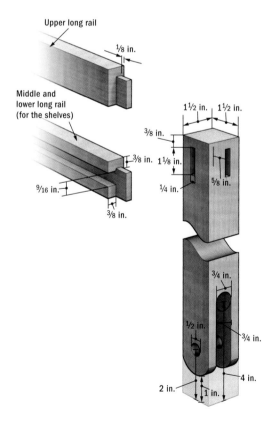

Stock Preparation

All of the parts are cut from a 2-in.-thick, 7-in.-wide, 10-ft.-long plank. Always start the milling process by cutting an inch or two off the end of your plank to ensure no checks or debris remain.

To start the rough milling, cut the board into three lengths of 36 in. Next, mill to 1⅝-in. thickness. You'll then want to cut out your parts: The legs are 1⅝ in. square; the rails are ⅞ in. thick; and the slats are rough milled to ¾ in. thick. Sticker the boards and let them sit at least overnight, allowing them to acclimate to your space. The following day, mill the parts to their finished dimensions (for now, leave the slats at their rough-mill thickness). Remove all millmarks (as needed) with a bench plane.

The rough-milling process is described in more detail on p. 7.

Making the parts

One of the best aspects of this project is seeing the beautifully figured pieces for the legs, rails, and slats emerge from an ordinary-looking plank of flatsawn maple. After the plank has been milled, the annual growth rings are tangential to the face (**photo 1**). This is flatsawn lumber, and it's not very exciting visually.

When the pieces for the project are milled from this blank, however, the growth rings will be perpendicular to the face. This quartersawn lumber really shows off the characteristic striping of tiger maple (**photo 2**).

Once the pieces are cut and milled to their finished dimensions, choose the legs based on how you want to position the grain. The striping on the two front legs of our piece resembles a herringbone pattern (**photo 3**). The pieces with less attractive grain can go elsewhere.

T-Mac Tip

Once you select the legs and determine how you want them placed on the cart (in the front or back), group them together and mark a triangle on the top end spanning all four legs. No matter how they're mixed up later on, you can always re-create their original orientation.

Mortising the legs

The legs have three mortises on each inside face: one at the top of the leg for the top rail and two lower ones for the rails that support the slats. The two lower sets of mortises can be adjusted up or down to create any shelf height you want.

Mark the top mortise. Lay out the top mortise. It starts $3/8$ in. down from the top of the leg. It's $1/4$ in. wide and $1^{1}/8$ in. long, and it starts $7/16$ in. from the outside face of the leg (**photo 1**).

Lay out the lower mortises. The other pairs of mortises should be marked where you want the shelves to fall. I started these at $12^{1}/2$ in. and 26 in. down from the top of the legs (**photo 2**).

Cut the mortises. Using a mortising machine (or whatever method you prefer), cut the mortises to a depth of $5/8$ in. Clean up the inside faces with a bench chisel and remove any remaining debris (**photo 3**).

T-Mac Tip

When setting your chisel into the mortiser, use a small square to make sure your chisel is square to the fence. Doing so makes for a clean mortise and allows for quick and easy cleanup at the bench.

Visiting a Countertop Fabricator

Paul D'Attanasio, the brother of *Rough Cut* shop mate Al D'Attanasio, introduced us to the three most popular types of countertops: man-made quartz composite, granite, and solid surface.

The composite is 93% quartz and 7% resin (shown at left). Granite is, of course, natural stone, and solid surface is made from plastic resin and other materials but can look like stone.

In addition to the piece of quartz that we selected for this project, Paul's shop also cut out a piece of solid surface that could be used. The slab was 30 in. wide and 10 ft. long, and the piece was given an ogee edge profile with a router.

One of the nice things about the solid surface material is that it can be cut using standard woodworking tools. It's also fairly heavy—our small top weighed about 35 lb.

Once the edges have been eased and profiled, the top is complete and ready for use. We took both the solid-surface and the quartz tops back to the shop to see which one visually fit best with our cart. (It was a toss-up—both looked great.)

Above: Man-made composite consisting mostly of quartz.

Right: Samples of quartz composite, granite, and solid surface.

Solid surface can be machined with standard woodworking tools.

A finished top ready for installation.

Making the rails

Sort through the rail pieces and choose the best pieces to be used in the most prominent places on the cart. Save the two highly figured pieces for the rails on the front of the cart (**photo 1**). Make sure to mark the faces, indicating which is the top and which is the bottom rail (**photo 2**).

Lay out the tenons for the rails. On the end of the rails, lay out the tenons. They are $5/8$ in. long and $1/4$ in. wide with a $1/8$-in. shoulder on the outside face. There's another shoulder $3/8$ in. from the top (**photo 3**).

Mark the groove. On the inside faces of the two lower sets of rails lay out a $9/16$-in.-wide groove that will accept the ends of the slats. To determine the location of the groove, measure up roughly $1/2$ in. from both the top and bottom edge of the rail to the edge of the groove. Your goal is to center the slat onto the rail (**photo 4**).

Cut the tenons for the rails. Set up the tablesaw with a stack dado $9/16$ in. wide, which can be used to groove the inside of the rails as well as cut the tenons. Start by cutting the $1/8$-in. shoulder on the outside faces of the rails (**photo 5**), then flip the rails over and set the dado height just below the layout line (**photo 6**). Make a cut and test the fit. Sneak up on a snug fit, and be careful not to make the tenons too loose for the mortises. Then cut the $3/8$-in. shoulders on the tops of the rails.

Cut the groove in the rails.

Using the same dado set, adjust the fence and the blade height and then run the inside faces of the long lower rails over the dado to make a groove $9/16$ in. wide and $3/8$ in. deep.

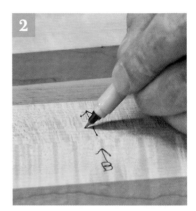

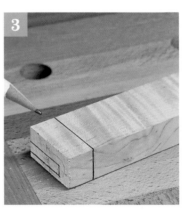

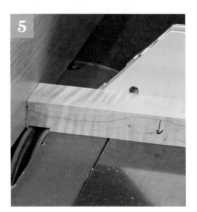

Clean up the grooves. The grooves may not be perfectly flat when the rails come off the tablesaw. Use a router plane set to $3/8$ in. to make sure the bottom of each groove is flat (**photo 7**).

Dry-fit the tenons. It's best to test-fit all of the tenons into their respective mortises, making any adjustments with a shoulder plane as necessary. Mark the location of the pieces as you go (**photo 8**).

Adding the slats

Dry-fit the base of the cart and clamp the pieces together, then measure for the slats that will form the two shelves.

Select for figure. There are 10 slats for each shelf. Lay them out on the bench and look for a grain pattern that's pleasing to your eye. I arranged the slats so the striping of the tiger maple created a herringbone pattern. Number the ends of the slats to keep them in order (**photo 1**).

Remove millmarks. Clean up the slats with a handplane to remove any millmarks or tearout. Then bring the slats to their finished thickness, either with a thickness planer or a handplane, and cut them to their correct length.

Assembling the shelves

The slats should be spaced evenly along the rails, separated by blocks of wood the same thickness as the slats and as deep as the groove. To make the spacing come out evenly, the blocks for this cart are 1¼ in. long.

Start at the center. After making a number of spacer blocks, find the center point of a rail and a block and then glue the block in, lining up the two centerlines. Take care not to use too much glue (**photo 1**).

Alternate slats and blocks. Working out from the center, add a slat (without glue) and spacer blocks (with glue) until all the blocks have been added (**photo 2**). Then remove the slats.

Plane the inside edge. When the glue has dried, the tops of the blocks may protrude slightly and the end blocks will overlap the tenons slightly (**photo 3**). Use a handplane to flatten the inside faces of the rails, and use a fine-tooth saw to trim away any excess at the ends of the rail.

Assemble the shelves. When all of the surfaces have been cleaned up, the slats can be put back in their proper locations and the shelves assembled.

Shopmade Wheels for Furniture

At the bottom of the two front legs are wheels set into recesses and pinned with wood dowels. You don't have to buy wheels. Instead, make them by gluing up blanks from three plies of ¼-in.-thick material and shaping them with a jig on the bandsaw.

Cut three pieces of ¼-in. stock 4½ in. square and glue them together so the grain alternates 90 degrees in adjacent pieces—just like a piece of plywood. Draw a 4-in. circle on the blank

(photo 1). Then drill a ½-in. hole in the center of the blank.

Make the jig by drilling a ½-in. hole 2 in. from the end of a piece of plywood and inserting a dowel in the hole. Place the wheel blank on the dowel, clamp the jig to the bandsaw table, and cut out the wheel (photo 2). Round over the square edges of the wheel and sand them smooth.

Next, drill a ¾-in. hole in the center of each leg 4 in. up from the bottom with the hole parallel to the long rails. Drill a ½-in. hole for the axle 2 in. up from the bottom, parallel to the short rails (photo 3). Now cut 1 in. from the bottom of the two front legs to give the wheels clearance.

To make room for the wheels, remove the material below the ¾-in. hole. You can start the cuts on the tablesaw and finish them on the bandsaw, then clean up the inside of the cuts if necessary and round the bottom corners of the leg (photo 4).

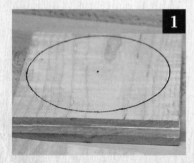

Assembly and finish

Glue up the sides. Glue the short sides of the cart together, making sure the slotted legs are oriented correctly (**photo 1**).

Add the wheels. Once the glue has dried, it's time to mount the wheels. Put a spot of glue in one side of the leg at the axle hole, insert a wheel, and drive in the dowel (**photo 2**). Before fully seating the dowel, add another spot of glue to the trailing end of the dowel and then drive it all the way in. The idea is to add glue for the axle so the glue is forced away from the center of the leg as the dowel is driven in.

Add the shelves. Glue the shelf assemblies and upper rails into one of the short sides, then glue on the other short side (**photo 3**). When all of the pieces are in place, clamp the cart together.

Finish the base. After cleaning up any glue residue and sanding the cart, add the finish of your choice. We brought out the figure of the tiger maple with a coat of linseed oil followed by several coats of lacquer buffed with steel wool (**photo 4**).

Put on the top. In the end, we settled on the quartz top. To mount it, we applied a bead of silicone to the top edge of the top rails, clamped the quartz in place, and let the silicone cure (**photo 5**).

DROP-LEAF TABLE

Making Hinged Fly Rails

Drop-leaf tables have been made in many sizes and styles, ranging from William and Mary to Shaker. But they all have one thing in common: versatility. When not in use, their leaves can be left down, so the table can be tucked up against a wall. When a larger surface is needed, one or both leaves can be secured in the up position.

This drop-leaf table is a good project for beginners. It consists of relatively few parts: four tapered legs, rails to connect them, and a simple, hinged top.

What makes building this project particularly interesting and fun is learning how to make the hinged fly rails that swing out to support the leaves. The challenge is to cut the interlocking parts to create

a hinge that not only opens and closes smoothly but also maintains a straight edge to support the leaf in a level position.

The top of this table is made from California big leaf maple, which has an exciting grain pattern. The base of the table is soft maple, but it could also be built from whatever wood you have available locally.

Aside from the hinged fly rails, the joints are all standard mortise and tenon, keeping construction relatively simple. Unlike some drop-leaf designs, this one does not use a rule joint to marry the leaves to the top. Instead, the leaves are left square-edged and joined to the center section with brass hinges.

Drop-Leaf Table

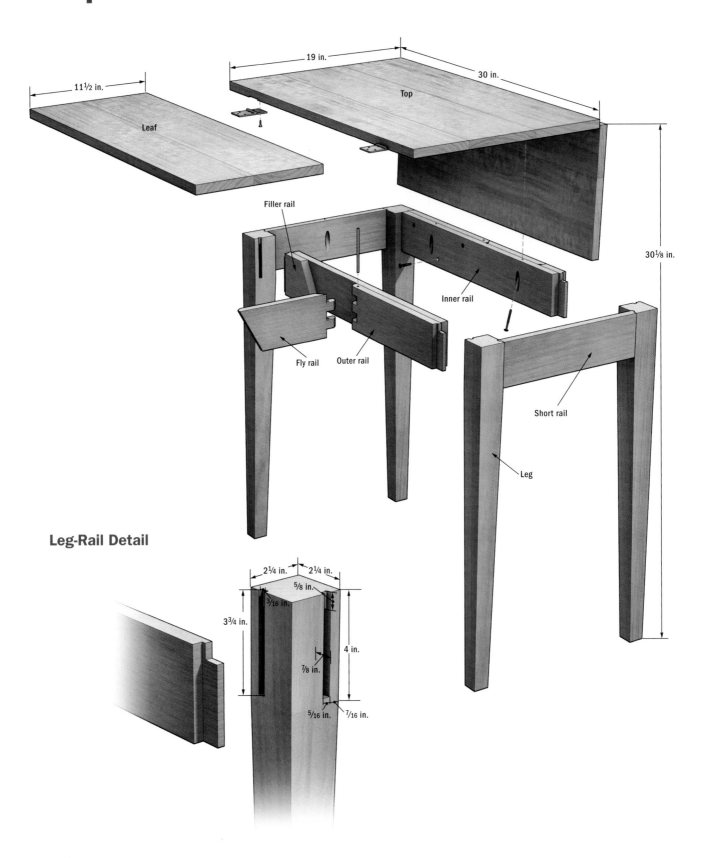

11½ in.

Leaf

19 in.

Top

30 in.

30⅛ in.

Filler rail

Inner rail

Fly rail

Outer rail

Short rail

Leg

Leg-Rail Detail

2¼ in.

2¼ in.

⅝ in.

³⁄₁₆ in.

3¾ in.

4 in.

⅞ in.

⁵⁄₁₆ in.

⁷⁄₁₆ in.

MATERIALS LIST/ROUGH MILL

PART	# OF PIECES	LENGTH (IN.)	WIDTH (IN.)	THICKNESS (IN.)	WOOD	NOTES
Legs	4	21⅜	2⅜	2⅜	Primary	
Short Rails	2	16¼	4¼	⅞	Primary	
Inner Rails	2	24½	4¼	⅞	Primary	
Outer Rails	2	29	4¼	⅞	Primary	
Top	1	31	19½	⅞	Primary	
Leaves	2	31	12	⅞		
Hinge Pins	2					3/16-in.-dia. brass or steel rod
Hinges	4					1½-in. x 2⅞-in. brass rule joint hinges
Screws	8					#8 x 2¼ in.

After cutting pieces to their rough lengths and widths, go through the rough milling process and sticker the pieces overnight. Then bring them to their finished dimensions the following day, following the steps that are explained in more detail on p. 7.

TOOL LIST

POWER TOOLS
Bandsaw
Cordless drill
Jointer
Mortising machine
Router
Tablesaw
Thickness planer

HAND TOOLS
Bench plane
Chisels
Marking gauge

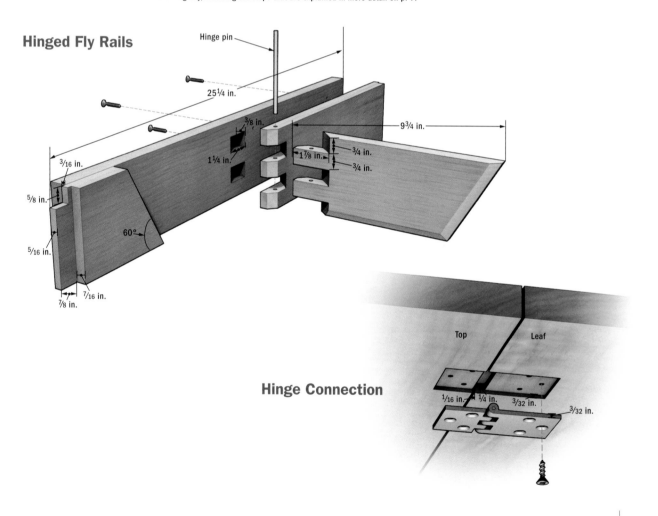

Hinged Fly Rails

Hinge pin

25¼ in.

9¾ in.

3/16 in.

⅝ in.

5/16 in.

60°

⅞ in.

7/16 in.

⅜ in.

1¼ in.

1⅞ in.

¾ in.

¾ in.

Hinge Connection

Top

Leaf

1/16 in.

¼ in.

3/32 in.

3/32 in.

Historic Tables in Boston

Top: A William and Mary table built in the first half of the 18th century.

Above: A "gate leg" design, with legs that swing outward to support the top when raised.

The Museum of Fine Arts in Boston, Massachusetts, has a number of drop-leaf tables in its American collection, including the gate-leg table at left, built sometime between 1710 and 1740.

This table is made in the early baroque style, also called the William and Mary style, characterized by turned legs that actually derive from the Dutch style. In addition to the four supporting legs, there are two additional legs that are housed in a half-lap joint cut into the base when the side leaves are in their down position. When the leaves are open, the legs swing out on a pivot point that supports them. These legs are commonly referred to as "gate legs."

Another table in the museum's collection, dating back to around 1785, is attributed to John Townsend of Newport, Rhode Island, considered one of the most well-known furniture makers of his time. The table has beautifully carved fretwork supports and reeded legs.

When a leaf is hinged up, it's supported by a fly rail, just like the one on the drop-leaf table we're building.

A drop-leaf table attributed to John Townsend of Newport, Rhode Island.

Fly rails support the raised top.

Making the legs

Before laying out any joinery, use a handplane to remove all millmarks. Next, lay out the mortises at the tops of the legs. They are $7/8$ in. deep, $5/16$ in. wide, and $3\frac{3}{4}$ in. long. They also have a $5/8$-in.-long, $3/16$-in.-deep haunch at the top and are set in from the outside edge of the leg by $7/16$ in.

Lay out the mortises. Set a combination square to the length of the mortise and mark the end (**photo 1**), then use a marking gauge to mark the outer edge of the mortise (**photo 2**). Reset the marking gauge and lay out the other edge of the mortise, then lay out the haunch.

Cut the mortises. Using a mortising machine or a router and jig, cut the mortises to the lines carefully (**photo 3**).

Lay out a taper. Mark the taper on the two inside faces of each leg. The taper starts 4 in. down from the top of the leg, and the leg tapers from the full thickness of your leg blank at the top down to $1\frac{3}{8}$ in. at the bottom. The end result is that you'll have taken off $7/8$ in. from the two inside faces of each leg.

Make a tapering jig. Make a jig to cut the tapers on the tablesaw by ripping a piece of plywood or medium-density fiberboard (MDF) to about 6 in. wide. Lay the leg on the MDF with the taper line aligned to the edge and trace the taper onto the MDF. Cut the MDF along this line. The jig can be open at the front end and has a stop point at the other, giving the leg a secure place to rest while cutting at the tablesaw (**photo 4**). If you don't want to make a jig, just mark and cut out the taper of the legs at the bandsaw. Either way, you'll still need to clean up the sawmarks.

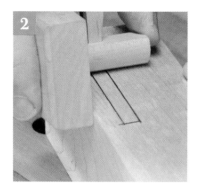

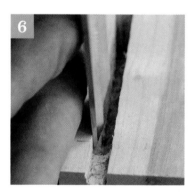

Cut the legs. Fit the leg into the jig, adjust the rip fence so the blade hits outside the taper mark, and run both inside faces over the blade (**photo 5**). Be mindful of which face is tapered first so that the leg rests on a flat face for both cuts. Clean up millmarks with a handplane.

Clean up the mortises. Using a narrow bench chisel, clean up any debris in the bottom of the mortise. Then, with a wide chisel, pare the side walls of the mortises to remove any roughness left from the mortiser (**photo 6**).

Making a Hinge in Wood

The long rails of this table consist of two parts—an inner rail that spans the whole distance from leg to leg and a shorter outer rail hinged in the middle. Mill the pieces to ¾ in. thick and 3¾ in. wide, but for now leave them a little long. Cut the outer rail in half at 90 degrees.

The goal in laying out the joint is to establish three key points: the chamfer on the ends of the fingers, the center point where the hinge pin goes in, and the back bevel that gives the hinge clearance as it opens and closes **(photo 1)**.

To lay out the chamfer locations, set a marking gauge to half the thickness of the rail (in this case, ⅜ in.) and scribe first the end and then the face of the rail **(photo 2)**. Using the same setting, scribe a line at the center of the rail **(photo 3)**. Mark both sides of the joint the same way.

To establish the pivot point for the pin, use a combination square to connect the two lines you've just scribed **(photo 4)**. Then flip the square around and make another 45-degree line that intersects the centerline **(photo 5)**.

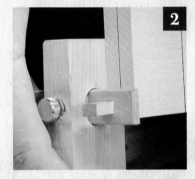

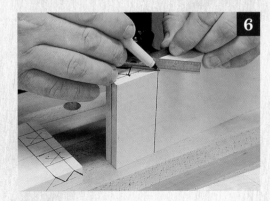

Flip the square once more and draw a line to establish the point where the joint will come together. Finally, lay out the back bevel **(photo 6).**

Divide the rail into five equal sections (in this case ¾ in.) and lay out the locations of the fingers across the width of both halves of the joint. Mark both sides of each board before changing the setting on your marking gauge. The joint is now ready to be cut **(photo 7).**

Using a ½-in.-wide dado, remove the waste between the fingers **(photo 8)**, then make a series of relief cuts to remove material on the back of the joint **(photo 9).** Be careful not to go past the shoulder line.

Using a regular blade set at 45 degrees and an L-fence attached to the rip fence, cut the chamfers to the layout lines **(photo 10).** Clean up the inside of the fingers so the joint fits together snugly, and be careful not to remove too much material **(photo 11).** Check to be sure that the assembled rail is straight **(photo 12).** If it's not, the fly rail will rise or fall as it swings out.

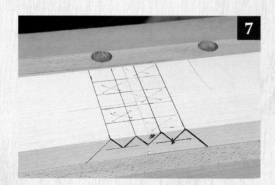

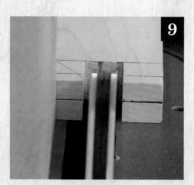

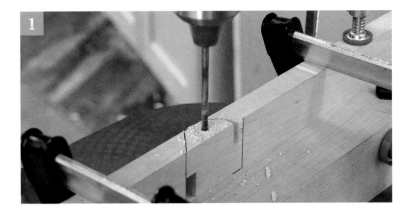

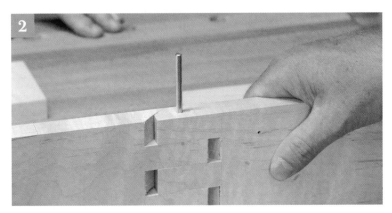

Completing the joint

Drill the pivot hole. Once the hinge has been fitted, take the assembled joint to the drill press, clamp it to the table, and drill the hole for the pivot pin on the layout mark (**photo 1**). The hole should be the same diameter as the pin. Drill halfway through, flip the board end for end, keeping the same face of the rail against the fence, and complete the hole. Assemble the joint and drive the pin most of the way in to check the fit (**photo 2**).

    Mark the inner rail. Mark the center point of one of the inner rails and clamp the three-fingered side of the outer rail so the pivot hole is aligned with the mark (**photo 3**). Mark the inside of the fingers on the inner rail (**photo 4**), making sure you also mark the back of the relief cut. Assemble the other half of the rail at 90 degrees, and mark where the ends of the fingers intersect the inner rail (**photo 5**).

T-Mac Tip

An easy way to remove the pivot pin as you work on the joint is with a cordless drill. Tighten the chuck over the exposed portion of the pin and back the pin out.

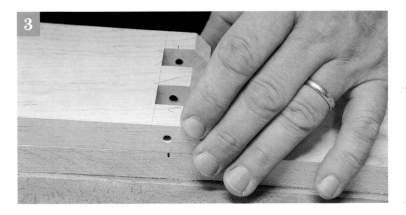

Chop out the mortises. The layout lines on the inner rail (**photo 6**) show the locations of mortises that will provide clearance for the fingers as they pivot and also act as a stop when the fly rail is perpendicular to the inner rail. Chop out the mortises to a depth of about ½ in. (**photo 7**).

Assemble the rail. Glue the permanent side of the joint to the inner rail, reinforcing the connection with screws driven from the inside of the inner rail. Cut the fly rail to length, 9¾ in. at a 60-degree angle, as shown in the drawing on p. 59. Save the cutoff as the filler piece at the end of the rail and glue it into place.

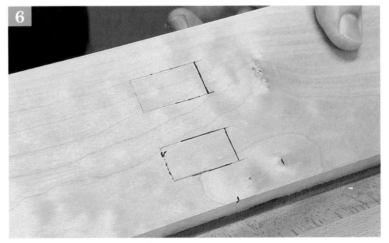

Cutting the tenons

Cut the rails to length. Mark the long rail to length with the pivot at the center of the rail, then cut the rail to length, 25¼ in. Cut the short rails to 15¼ in.

Lay out the tenons. Set a marking gauge to ⅞ in. and mark the ends of the rails across their faces (**photo 1**). Reset the marking gauge to ⁷⁄₁₆ in., which is the setback from the edge of the leg to where the mortise begins, and scribe the top of the rail (**photo 2**). The short rails are marked in exactly the same way.

Cut the tenons. Set up a ⅞-in. dado on the tablesaw and raise the height of the blade to ⁷⁄₁₆ in. Cut the outside faces of all four rails (**photo 3**). On the long rails, reset the height of the dado so it just meets the back of the outer rail and remove the remaining waste (**photo 4**). Creep up to the line, checking the fit as you go along to avoid taking off too much material.

Clean up the tenons. At the bench, align the bottom of the tenon with the bottom of the mortise and mark the

haunch **(photo 5).** Cut away the waste with a fine-tooth saw.

Test the fit. The outside faces of the rails should now be flush with the leg **(photo 6).** If they're not, some fine-tuning can be done after the parts have been glued together.

T-Mac Tip

The haunch at the top of the tenon helps align the rail with the leg. It does not have to sit all the way into the mortise, so if there's a gap between the end of the haunch and the leg (as shown in photo 6 at right) don't worry about it. If the haunch is too long, it will prevent the shoulder from seating tightly against the leg.

Gluing up

Glue the short sides. With all of the tenons fitted into the legs, glue together the base of the table. Start with the short rails and legs, applying glue to both the mortises and tenons. Don't use too much glue—the excess will have to be cleaned up later **(photo 1)**. Clamp the short sides **(photo 2)**.

Complete the glue-up. After the short rails have been given time to dry, glue the long rails to complete the base. Make sure you check the base for square by measuring diagonally from one leg to the other and comparing that to the distance between the other two legs. If the distance is the same, the base is square. If not, you should be able to bring it into square by adjusting the clamping pressure or repositioning the clamp heads.

Making the top

Glue up the top. Once adjoining edges of the top are squared, clamp the adjacent boards face to face in the vise and plane a slight hollow in the edge, taking more material from the middle than the ends. Laid flat, the boards should touch only at the ends but should close in the middle with moderate clamping pressure. This is called a spring joint. Glue the boards together, flush up all the joints, and cut the top to its final dimensions. The top should overhang the base by 1/2 in. in width.

Add the leaves. Cut the leaves to their final dimensions and lay out the hinge locations. Hinges are 3 1/2 in. in from the ends of the top. The barrel of the hinge is set flush to the edge of the leaf. After knifing the width, length, and depth of the hinge leaves, carefully remove material until the hinge fits, then chop out space for the hinge barrels in the edges of the leaves (**photo 1**).

Screw the hinges in. When you screw the hinges into the mortises, make sure the screws aren't too long. For this ³⁄₄-in.-thick top, use ¹⁄₂-in. screws (**photo 2**).

Attach the top. Drill a half-dozen holes at an angle through the rails, center the top on the base, and screw through the holes into the top. Once again, make sure the screws aren't too long (**photo 3**).

Finish up. Clean up any dents, gouges, or glue residue, sand the surfaces, and apply your finish of choice according to the manufacturer's instructions. The finish we chose starts with aniline dye, which unified the different colors in the wood (**photo 4**). We followed that with several coats of lacquer, sanding in between each coat with 320-grit paper. The thickness of the finish can be built until you're satisfied with the sheen, then you should apply a final coat of colored wax.

T-Mac Tip

Aniline dye comes in both water- and alcohol-soluble versions. If you use water-soluble dye, it will raise the grain of the wood and roughen it slightly. Before applying the dye, go over the top with a damp cloth and allow the wood to dry. Knock down the raised grain with fine sandpaper, clear any dust from the surface, and then apply the dye.

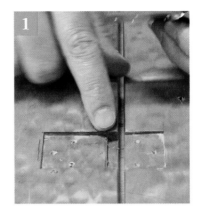

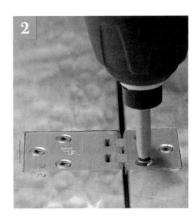

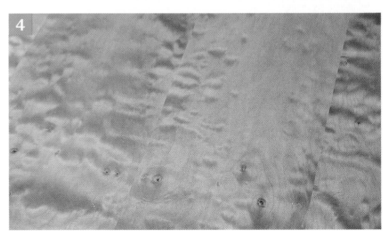

TURNED FLOOR LAMP

Learning the Basics of Turning

This lamp is the re-creation of a floor lamp that's been in my dad's den for 20 years. I love the turning because it covers all the basics—coves, beads, and flats. It also provides the opportunity for adaptations that will really make this project your own.

This lamp is turned in two sections that are connected with a mortise-and-tenon joint. It's in two sections because the lamp is 5 ft. tall and the lathe in my shop is only 42 in. between two centers. If you have a small lathe, you can still make this project; it will just require more sections and joinery. The base, which is a good exercise in face-turning, is mortised for a tenon in the lower section of the post.

At the top of the lamp is a turned wood shade made by a New Hampshire craftsman. The walls of the shade are turned really thin to allow light to pass right through, creating a warm, rich hue.

This lamp requires little material and few supplies to build. You'll need a finial and lamp kit, scrap plywood, and a modest amount of lumber. What's great about this project is that because it requires very little material, it lends itself to creative thinking at the lumberyard, where you might want to splurge on some figured or exotic material. I chose tiger maple, which I enhanced with a dramatic aniline dye.

Turned Floor Lamp

Post Details

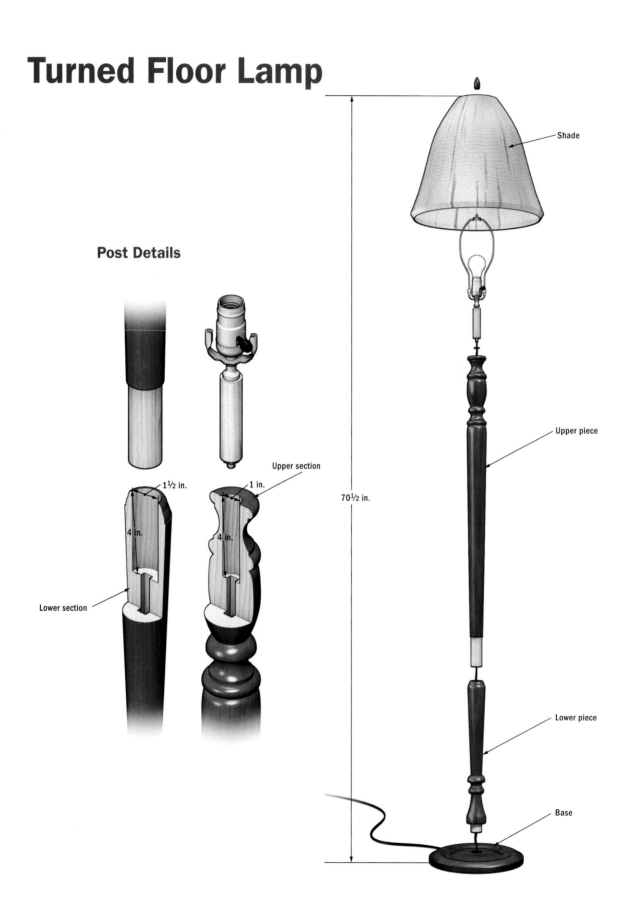

Upper section

1 in.

4 in.

Lower section

1½ in.

4 in.

Shade

Upper piece

Lower piece

Base

70½ in.

MATERIALS LIST/ROUGH MILL

PART	# OF PIECES	LENGTH (IN.)	WIDTH (IN.)	THICKNESS (IN.)	WOOD	NOTES
Lower Posts	2	21¼	2⅞	1⅜	Primary	
Upper Posts	2	42¾	2⅞	1⅜	Primary	
Base	3	14	5	1⅜	Primary	
Hardware Mount	1	10	1⅛	1⅛	Primary	
Plug	1	25	⅝	⅝	Secondary	
Lamp Hardware Kit	1					Threaded tube, nuts, wire, bulb socket, lampshade loop
Lampshade	1					
Finial	1					Optional; could be replaced by a nut
Plywood	1					8-in. x ¾-in. circle for faceplate

Go through the rough milling procedures as explained on p. 7. After stickering the parts overnight, finish-mill them and bring them all to their final dimensions provided in the materials list.

TOOL LIST

POWER TOOLS
Bandsaw
Drill
Jointer
Lathe
Miter saw
Tablesaw
Thickness planer

HAND TOOLS
Chisels
Glue scraper
Handplane

Turning Profile

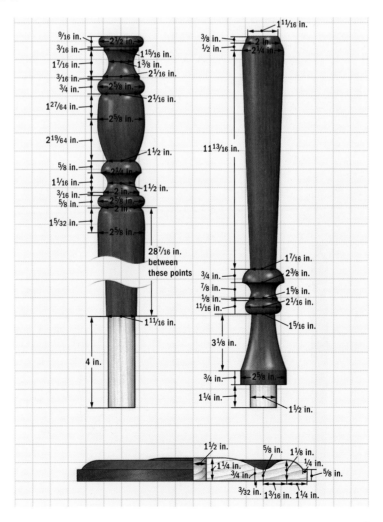

Making a Long Wire Chase

It takes nearly 6 ft. of lamp cord to get electricity from the floor to the bulb. Drilling out the center of the post for the cord would be nearly impossible, but there's an easy way of creating a wire chase inside the post—and it's done before the post is turned on the lathe.

The trick is to cut a groove in the center of the two pieces that will be glued together to create a post blank.

Start by setting up a ½-in. dado on the tablesaw with the height adjusted to ¼ in. At roughly the midpoint, cut a groove in both post pieces, working one at a time **(photo 1).** Flip each piece end for end and repeat the cuts. This centers the grooves in the boards. To ensure a nice, clean glue joint and almost invisible line, handplane the millmarks off the inside faces of the boards.

T-Mac Tip

Sort through the material before cutting the grooves, and hide any blemishes in the wood by orienting them toward the center of the post.

Apply glue to both inside faces of each pair of boards **(photo 2).** Don't apply too much glue, and keep as much as possible out of the grooves. Next, clamp each pair of pieces together, starting with a clamp in the middle, and allow the glue to dry for 24 hours **(photo 3).**

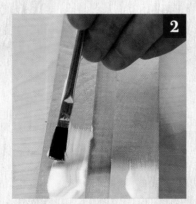

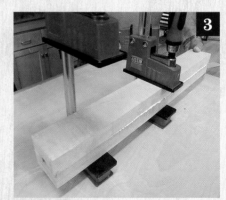

Getting ready to turn

Scrape off the glue. After the glue has dried, use a scraper to remove the residue (**photo 1**). There's no need to remove any millmarks from the surfaces with a handplane because the blanks will be turned on the lathe.

Size the parts. Cut the blanks to size on the miter saw by squaring one end, flipping the blank around, and cutting the other end to length, with one piece cut to 41¾ in. and the other piece cut to 20¼ in. (**photo 2**).

Knock off the corners. To make the square blank easier and safer to turn on the lathe, set the tablesaw blade to 45 degrees and take off about ⅝ in. at each corner (**photo 3**). This process will turn each square blank into an octagon.

Fill in the hole. Plug the ends of each blank with a piece of wood so the blank can be mounted on the lathe (**photo 4**). I glued in pieces of pine.

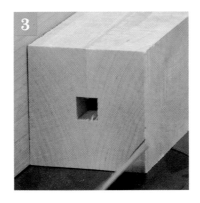

Visiting a Master Turner

One of the focal points of this lamp is the beautifully turned wooden lampshade made by New Hampshire craftsman Peter Bloch.

Bloch starts making this lampshade with a 20-in. section of aspen, which he cuts from the log with a chainsaw. On one end of the piece, he marks out the location of the face plate and then uses the chainsaw to slice away parts of the blank until it has a roughly cone-like shape. The blank is then hauled inside and mounted on the lathe.

After turning the blank to a smooth conical shape on the outside, Bloch tackles the inside. He gradually hollows out the blank, working first with a heavy-duty gouge and later switching to an arm-brace tool.

As the walls of the lampshade get thinner, he turns off all the lights in the shop except his work light and gauges his

Bloch kills the shop lights to gauge wall thickness based on translucence.

progress by how translucent the walls become. When he's finished, the walls will be about $\frac{1}{10}$ in. thick.

When the shade comes off the lathe, it will still need a lot of sanding, plus the addition of a plywood shade ring that allows the shade to be mounted to the lamp. Bloch treats the lampshade with three coats of a synthetic tung oil.

Above top: A 20-in. length of aspen worked into a roughly conical shape.

Above center: The blank mounted on the lathe, ready for turning.

Above bottom: Working the inside with a heavy gouge.

Right: The shade needs sanding straight off the lathe.

A plywood ring attaches the shade to the lamp.

Begin turning

After marking the post blanks' top and bottom (**photo 1**), find the center of the octagon and mark both the top and the bottom of each blank (**photo 2**).

Mount the blank in the lathe. Put the tip of the drive center in the center mark on the blank (**photo 3**) and tap it in with a hammer until the teeth are set firmly into the surface of the wood (**photo 4**). Insert the drive center into the headstock of the lathe, then engage the tailstock (**photo 5**). It doesn't have to be overly tight, but it should sit snugly and securely.

Test the setup. Turn on the lathe briefly just to make sure the blank is held firmly between the headstock and tailstock. It's a good idea to take a couple of steps back from the machine just in the case the blank flies out of the lathe.

Turn a cylinder. Adjust the tool rest and turn the blank into a cylinder, preserving as much of the material as you can (**photo 6**).

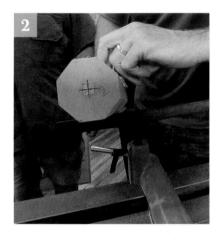

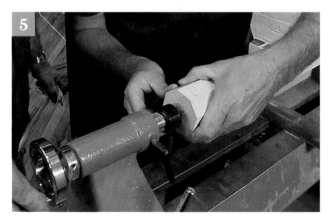

Shaping the columns

I copied an existing profile on the column (**photo 1**), but you could create any design you like.

Mark the blank. Start by making a pattern on a piece of ¼-in. plywood that shows the location of all the key points on the upper and lower posts. I hold the pattern against the column and transfer the marks to the blank (**photo 2**), working a few at a time. Steady a pencil on the tool rest on the marks you've just made and spin the blank by hand to transfer the outline of the design all the way around the column (**photo 3**).

T-Mac Tip

You only need to make a pattern for areas of the post that get turned details. This occurs at the top and the bottom of the post. The long midsection of smoothly tapered post doesn't need a pattern.

Cut the tenon. The two sections of post are joined with a mortise and tenon. On the bottom of the long blank, lay out the location for a 4-in.-long tenon. The tenon should be 1½ in. in diameter. To get a proper fit, drill a 1½-in. hole in a scrap of wood and use calipers to get the tenon close to 1½ in. Turn off the lathe, loosen the tailstock, and test the tenon in the scrap of wood. Continue this process until the tenon fits the hole snugly. On the bottom of the lower post, cut a 1½-in. tenon 1¼ in. long to fit the post into the base.

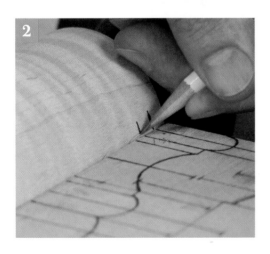

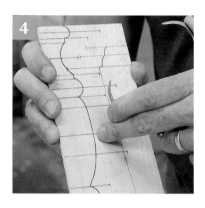

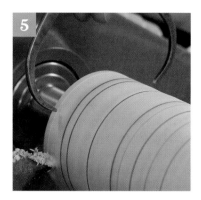

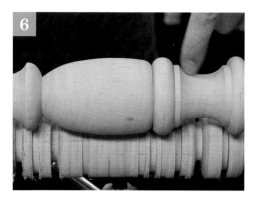

Set in the depths. Set the calipers to the diameter of the first key point on the column (**photo 4**) and then cut in the depth. Continue down the length of the column with a straight turning tool until all of the depths have been established (**photo 5**). Using multiple sets of calipers will make this job go a lot faster.

Round over the shapes. At this stage, the turning looks pretty rough (**photo 6**). The next step is to round over the rough edges to form the smooth contours of a finished post. Work slowly and carefully (**photo 7**), and choose the appropriate tool for the shape you're trying to create.

Sand the post. After you've refined all the shapes, sand the column to remove the tool marks. Don't use a grit any finer than 220 because it will burnish the surface and make it more difficult for your finish to penetrate the wood.

Drill out the mortises. In the top of the bottom post, drill a 1½-in.-dia., 4-in.-deep mortise by replacing the tailstock with a drill bit and slowly advancing the bit into the wood (**photo 8**). In the top of the upper post, drill a 1-in.-dia. by 4-in.-deep hole.

Making the base

The base of the lamp is a 13-in. round. On a piece of 1¼-in. material that's slightly bigger than 13 in., use a pair of dividers to draw a 13-in. circle. Working from the same center point, draw an 8-in. circle. This will be used to locate an 8-in.-dia. plywood mounting block, which gives the turning more stability (**photo 1**). You'll then want to screw the plywood into the blank and attach the metal face plate with 1¼-in. screws.

Cut out the circle. Cut out the blank on the bandsaw, making sure to stay outside the line (**photo 2**).

Turn the base. Mount the blank on the lathe, true up the edge, and then true up the face (**photo 3**).

Transfer your patterns. Lay out lines onto the face of the base, then turn the profiles (**photo 4**). Once the turning is done and the base has been sanded, drill a 1½-in. hole in the center of the base using the same technique as you did on the column (**photo 5**).

Assemble the lamp. Do a dry run to make sure any clamping issues are sorted out. Use a drill and chisel to remove the plugs in the ends of each piece, and make sure the post sits squarely to the base. Make any adjustments necessary.

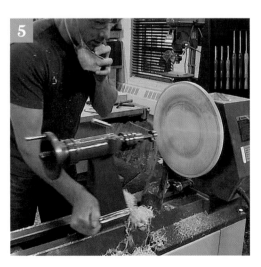

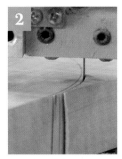

Finishing up

Assemble the hardware. Turn the mounting plug for the top of the post and fit it to the hole (alternatively, you can buy a length of dowel). The plug is 4 in. long and 1 in. in diameter. Drill out the center of the mount to fit the threaded tube, then fit the tube into the mount and tighten a nut on each end. Thread the wire up through the post and through the tube, attach the wire to the socket, and assemble the remaining hardware following the manufacturer's instructions (**photo 1**).

Glue the lamp together. After the wire has been run through the post, glue the two post sections together and then glue the post into the base.

Remove glue residue. Clean off any glue residue and repair any tearout, dents, or gouges. Then sand any spots you may have missed earlier to get the surface ready for a finish.

Apply finish. Add the finish of your choice, following the manufacturer's instructions. I used a coat of red aniline dye, followed by several coats of high-gloss lacquer, sanding between coats with 320-grit paper. The finish really makes the lamp come alive (**photo 2**).

STANDING MIRROR

Cutting Dovetails

When I started to design this project I knew it was going to be a collaboration with California's Paul Schürch, a marquetry artist whose work I have always admired.

Marquetry is the creation of images with different wood veneers. For me, the most inspiring examples of marquetry came out of France during the late 1700s. So when it came to designing the mirror, my mind naturally drifted to France and the most iconic symbol of that country—the Eiffel Tower. I knew I had to incorporate this structure into my overall design. If you look at the side of the standing mirror, my hope is it will feel reminiscent of the Eiffel Tower.

This is a fairly simple project, consisting of a three-piece base in which a mirror frame pivots. The base is assembled with a dovetail joint, which is cut on the router table. The mitered mirror frame, reinforced with easy-to-make splines at the corners, is capped by a beautiful marquetry design that I asked Paul to make in his shop.

The broad sides of the base also can be an opportunity for design adjustments of your own. You might, for example, introduce a contrasting veneer panel at the base that complements the marquetry on the top of the frame (see Design Options on p. 93).

I chose cherry for this project, but walnut, oak, maple, and other hardwoods would work just as well.

Standing Mirror

Sides

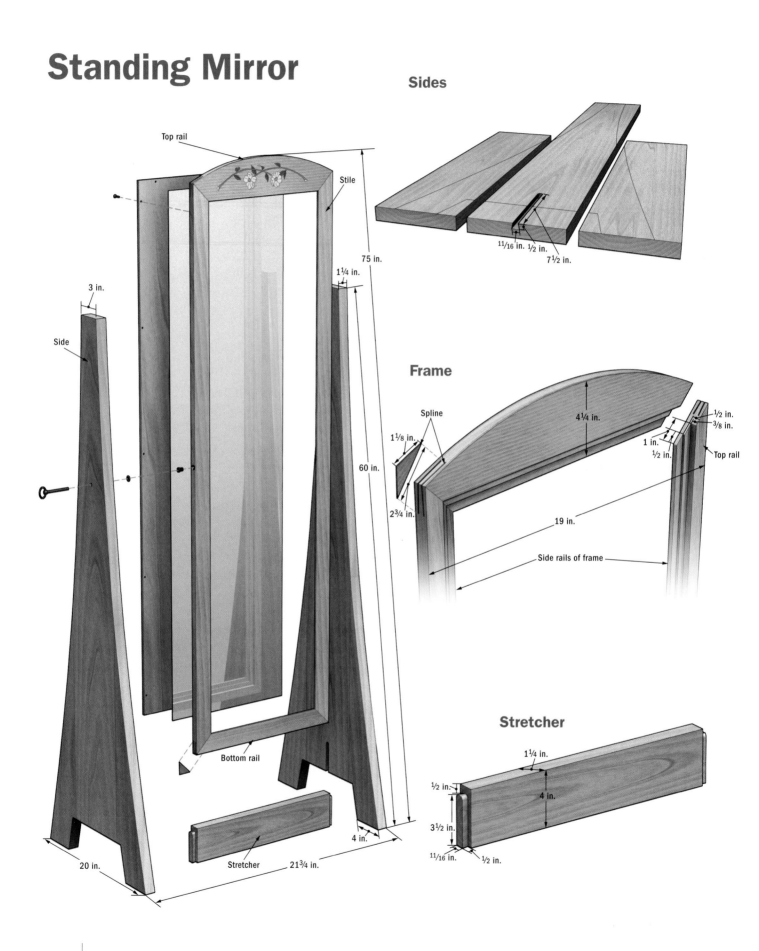

Top rail

Stile

75 in.

1¹⁄₄ in.

60 in.

3 in.

Side

Bottom rail

Stretcher

21³⁄₄ in.

20 in.

4 in.

¹¹⁄₁₆ in.   ¹⁄₂ in.

7¹⁄₂ in.

Frame

Spline

1¹⁄₈ in.

2³⁄₄ in.

4¹⁄₄ in.

1 in.

¹⁄₂ in.

¹⁄₂ in.

³⁄₈ in.

Top rail

19 in.

Side rails of frame

Stretcher

1¹⁄₄ in.

¹⁄₂ in.

4 in.

3¹⁄₂ in.

¹¹⁄₁₆ in.   ¹⁄₂ in.

MATERIALS LIST/ROUGH MILL

PART	# OF PIECES	LENGTH (IN.)	WIDTH (IN.)	THICKNESS (IN.)	WOOD	NOTES
Sides	2	61	20½	1⅜	Primary	
Stretcher	1	21¹/₁₄	4½	1⅜	Primary	
Stiles	2	63¾	2½	⅞	Primary	
Bottom Rail	1	20	2½	⅞	Primary	
Top Rail	1	20	4¾	¹¹/₁₆	Primary	
Splines	2	14	1⅝	¾	Primary	
Primary Veneer	2	20	20			
Pattern Veneer	1 of each color	20	4½			
Mirror Frame Hardware	1 pair					Knobs, threaded rod, frame attachments
Plywood Back	1	60¾	17	¼		
Screws	12					#6 x 1½ in.

Milling stock is a two-part process, which is explained in more detail on p. 7. In short, the pieces are cut to rough length, flattened on the jointer, and run through the thickness planer. After stickering the parts overnight, repeat the process to bring the parts to their finished dimensions.

TOOL LIST

POWER TOOLS
Bandsaw
Jigsaw
Router
Router table
Tablesaw
Thickness planer

HAND TOOLS
Bench chisels
Fine-tooth saw
Handplane
Soft-blow hammer

Marquetry

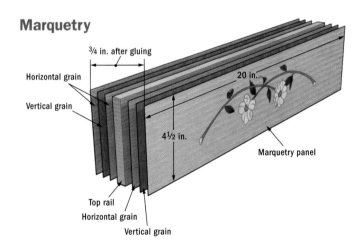

¾ in. after gluing

Horizontal grain

Vertical grain

20 in.

4½ in.

Marquetry panel

Top rail

Horizontal grain

Vertical grain

Top Rail

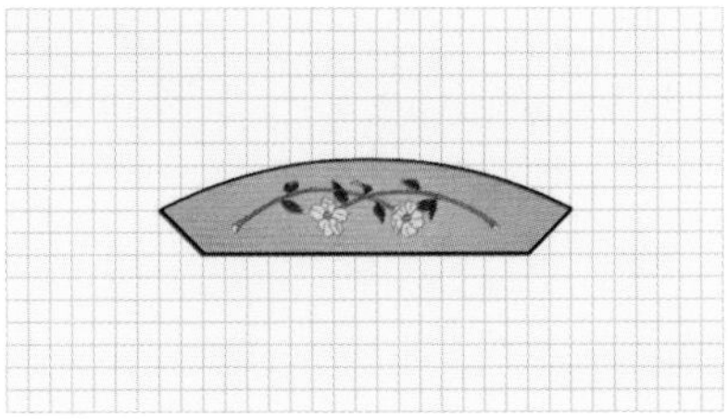

Side Pattern

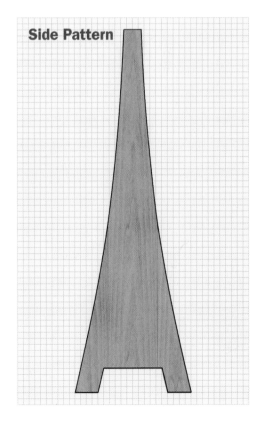

Making Dovetails

The stretcher connects the two sides of the mirror with a dovetail joint, which is laid out at the midpoint of each side **(photo 1).** Because the sides haven't been cut to shape yet, the socket is cut 7½ in. up from the bottom of the board. Later, the center portion of the board will be cut away to form the feet, leaving the dovetail socket 3½ in. long.

Set up the router table with a ¾-in. dovetail bit set ½ in. high and a stop block clamped 7½ in. away from the bit **(photo 2).** A second stop block clamped to the fence helps keep the stock from bobbling. Adjust the fence so the bit falls at the centerline.

Run the stock slowly up to the stop block, then pull it straight back until it clears the bit **(photo 3).**

To make the matching tails in the stretcher, start by finding the centerline and then laying out a ¾-in.-wide dovetail on each end **(photo 4).**

Leave the bit at the same height (½ in.) and use an auxiliary fence so only half the bit is exposed. Working at the router table, remove the material on one side of both ends, then flip the board around and remove the material on the other side. You'll want to creep up to the layout line until the joint fits snugly.

You'll still have to create the shoulder in the end of the joint. At the bench, cut away the top ½ in. of the tail and round the profile with a chisel so it will fit the socket **(photo 5).**

Laying out the sides

Make a pattern. Before any wood is cut, you need to make a pattern that is the full size of the sides. I made the sides of the mirror 3 in. wide at the top and 20 in. wide at the bottom, but feel free to make them whatever size you find appealing. Start with a piece of ³/₄-in. plywood 60 in. long and 20 in. wide and mark the centerline from top to bottom. To create the curve of the side, I came over 1¹/₂ in. from the centerline at the top and 10 in. from the centerline at the bottom; at roughly 10-in. intervals, I marked different points of the arc in between. Then, with the help of a thin piece of stock, I was able to create the curve by connecting all of the points (**photo 1**). There is no right or wrong in terms of the look of the curve, so make the project your own. The feet are 4 in. wide, with the inside curve following the one on the outside (**photo 2**). The cutout is 4 in. high. Cut to the lines on the bandsaw and fair the curves with a file and sandpaper.

Lay out the sides. The chances of finding a single board 20 in. wide for the sides are slim. Even if you could, cutting so much material away would produce a lot of waste. The stock I used was about 8¹/₂ in. wide. I cut the 8-ft.-long plank into two pieces, 5 ft. and 3 ft., and traced the center portion of the pattern on the longer board. I used the offcut to form the two wings at the bottom (**photo 3**). One face of the board allows enough for one side. The board is then turned over and flipped end for end, allowing enough material for the other side (**photo 4**). Those pieces are glued on later.

Making the sides

The three pieces that make up each side of the mirror have to be glued together. In each of the smaller pieces, cut a stair-step pattern along one edge (**photo 1**), giving the clamps two parallel surfaces that will provide even clamping pressure.

Glue up. Spread glue over the mating surfaces and apply even clamping pressure to draw the pieces together (**photo 2**). Check the bottom of the piece to make sure all three edges are flush. Put the pieces aside for an hour or two, allowing the glue to dry.

T-Mac Tip

To keep glue off your bench, use a piece of cardboard under your work.

Cut out the sides. Once the sides are all together, you'll find they are pretty heavy, which can make cutting them at the bandsaw more challenging. To make life easier, I decided to use a jigsaw at the bench (**photo 3**).

Cut out the bottom. Hang the piece over the end of the bench, clamp it in place, and use the jigsaw to cut out the feet at the bottom end of each side piece (**photo 4**).

Attach the pattern. Line up the centerline of the pattern with the centerline on a side piece and screw the two together using a few #8 by 1-in. screws **(photo 5)**. (The holes will be hidden by the frame.)

Flush-cut the sides. Now the sides can be trimmed to their final shape with a router and a bearing-guided bit **(photo 6).** Clamp a side to the bench so the edge is completely clear, and carefully flush-cut one side at a time **(photo 7).**

A Master of Marquetry

Paul Schürch has worked as a piano and organ builder, has studied boatbuilding in England, and even had a stint as a master carpenter aboard a schooner. But he is best known for the beautiful marquetry he creates at his shop in Santa Barbara, California.

The art of marquetry is doable even for people who don't draw very well. Paul starts the process with a photocopy from a book and loosely traces the design he wants to create on an overlay that matches the shape and size of the piece.

After making the pattern and numbering the parts, he stacks up all of the various pieces of veneer that will become part of the image and pins them to a piece of cardboard.

Using a scrollsaw, Paul cuts out all of the pieces. After all the pieces are cut, each stack of pieces is set to the side.

Once the pattern is completely cut out, he sorts through the veneer and finds his background layer, which he then temporarily covers with painter's tape. Next, he flips it over and builds the image with the pieces he cut out on the scrollsaw.

On the other side, Paul puts paper gum tape down, securing all of the pieces to the backer veneer. He then flips the piece back over again, removes the painter's tape, and then glues the finished image to two pieces of backer veneer. When the glue has dried, he dampens the gum tape and scrapes it off the surface, revealing the image. Once the piece has dried, Paul gives it a light sanding.

Tracing the pattern on an overlay.

Left top: Stacked veneer pinned to cardboard.

Left center and bottom: Cutting out with a scrollsaw.

Right top: Background layer covered with painter's tape.

Right center: Creating the image with pieces of veneer.

Right bottom: The finished design, glued to backer veneer and lightly sanded.

Assembly

Apply glue and assemble. Lay one side flat on the bench, apply glue to both sides of the joint (**photo 1**), and use a soft-blow hammer to drive the stretcher until the joint is fully seated (**photo 2**).

Add the second side. Apply glue to the back end of the other stretcher tail (**photo 3**) and on the inside of the corresponding socket. Clamp the side piece to the bench to keep it from moving around, then lift the other side piece into place and drive the two together (**photo 4**).

Clamp up the base. Stand the base upright on the bench and check to make sure that all four feet sit evenly, then clamp the base together (**photo 5**). Be careful not to use too much pressure so you don't distort the sides. If there's a small gap between the stretcher and side, don't worry about it. Most of that will be hidden by the mirror frame.

Make sure the sides are parallel. Measure the distance between the two sides at the stretcher and again at the top of the base to make sure the two sides are parallel. If not, make an adjustment with a clamp at the top (**photo 6**).

Making the frame

Glue up the top rail. The marquetry that Paul made will be glued to a $9/16$-in.-thick core. To prevent the piece from warping, an equal amount of veneer is glued to the back. For this counterveneer, layer three pieces, alternating the direction of the grain, and glue the whole blank together (**photo 1**). It's now the same thickness as the other pieces in the frame.

Cut the rabbets. There are two rabbets cut into the back of all four frame pieces. One holds the mirror and the second holds the plywood back (**photo 2**). The rabbet for the mirror leaves a $1/4$-in.-thick reveal on the front of the frame. Cut the rabbets on the tablesaw.

Cut the miters. Miter the four frame pieces, but note that the top rail doesn't get mitered all the way to the top corners because it's wider than the sides and bottom. Stop the miter 2 in. up from the bottom edge.

Glue on clamping blocks. To make it easy to apply even pressure across the miter with clamps, cut glue blocks to a 45-degree angle and glue to each corner (**photo 3**). Apply glue to both sides of all the joints, then glue up the frame.

Remove the blocks. After the glue has dried, use a chisel to remove most of each block, working in carefully from the outside (**photo 4**). Clean up the last bit with a handplane.

Shape the top rail. Draw a curve on the top of the top rail (**photo 5**). Cut out the shape with a jigsaw or at the bandsaw and clean up the cut with a file and sandpaper.

Spline the corners. Using a fine-tooth handsaw, cut two kerfs at a slight angle at each corner **(photo 6)**, then glue in pieces of veneer **(photo 7)**. When the glue has dried, trim the veneer flush to the frame.

Mount the frame. The mirror frame is held between the two sides with a threaded post and a threaded insert **(photo 8)**. Find the center point of the frame by balancing it on pencils or dowels, then drill holes for the threaded pin in the frame. Measure the distance from the bottom of the frame to the holes, add 2 in. to this dimension, and mark the sides (this gives the mirror some clearance to swing). Drill the holes in the sides and attach the hardware.

Finishing up

Fit the ¼-in. plywood back for the frame, carving out some room for the hardware if necessary, and predrill holes for screws along the edges. Then clean up all surfaces and apply the finish of your choice following the manufacturer's directions. I used boiled linseed oil to bring out the color of the cherry, followed by several coats of shellac.

After the finish has dried, put the mirror in. Lay the face frame face down on the bench, with a blanket between the two for protection, and then carefully lay the mirror in place. Secure the plywood back using #6 by ½-in. screws.

DESIGN Options

ONE WAY OF LIGHTENING UP the look of the mirror is to add panels at the bottom of each side in a slightly contrasting wood. I book-matched some highly figured veneer for this spot, but you could even go with a colored veneer that would complement the colors in the marquetry.

VENEERED COFFEE TABLE

Working with Veneer

This project is an opportunity to combine two versatile materials—steel and wood.

The top of the table is made from a decorative camphor burl veneer, which is glued to a pine substrate. The base is light-gauge steel that's been shaped, welded, and powder-coated at my local metal fabrication shop.

Veneer is available in many exotic species of wood. It is created by cutting a solid piece of wood into thin sheets that are only about $1/42$ in. thick and stacked sequentially into what is called a "flitch." The thin sheets not only allow the material to be used efficiently but also provide flexibility in design because the pieces have almost identical grain patterns. This affords you the freedom to create mirrored patterns with matching grains.

The design possibilities are limited only by your imagination.

Working with veneer can present some challenges. You may find that the sheets are brittle, depending on the grain patterns or figure in the wood. If they are, you will need to treat them with veneer softener before working with them. For this project, the veneer will be applied to a solid pine core that is constructed to minimize wood movement. A piece of plywood or medium-density fiberboard (MDF) will also do the trick.

The metal base presented an opportunity to do some great design work. If your tastes are more traditional, however, or if a metal shop just isn't convenient, you can design something dramatic out of wood (see Design Options on p. 97).

Veneered Coffee Table

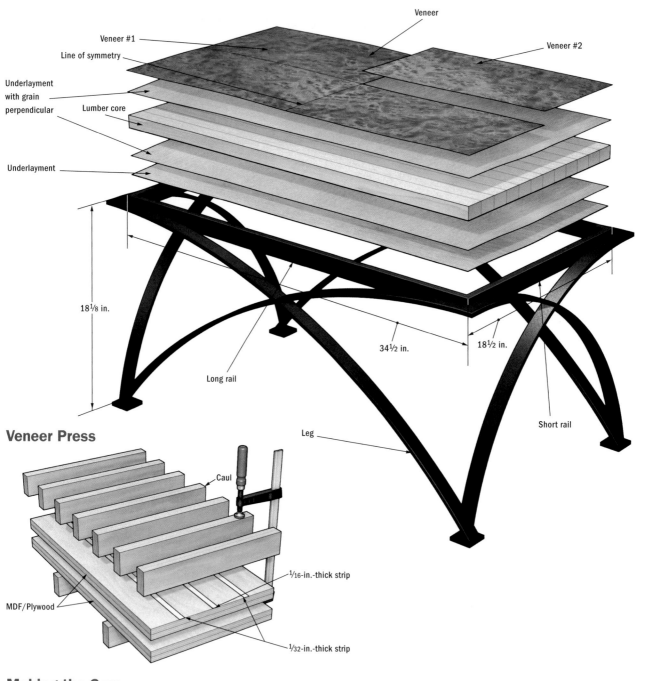

Veneer

Veneer #1

Veneer #2

Line of symmetry

Underlayment
with grain
perpendicular

Lumber core

Underlayment

18 1/8 in.

34 1/2 in.

18 1/2 in.

Long rail

Short rail

Leg

Veneer Press

Caul

1/16-in.-thick strip

MDF/Plywood

1/32-in.-thick strip

Making the Core

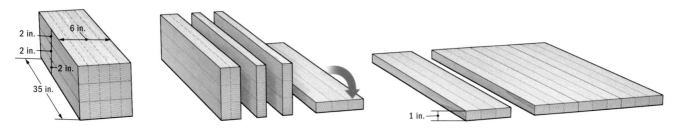

2 in.

6 in.

2 in.

2 in.

35 in.

1 in.

MATERIALS LIST/ROUGH MILL

PART	# OF PIECES	LENGTH (IN.)	WIDTH (IN.)	THICKNESS (IN.)	WOOD	NOTES
Top (Lumber Core)	3	35	6	2	Pine	
Long Edging	2	35½	1	1¼	Primary	
Short Edging	3	19½	1	1¼	Primary	
Legs	4	18	1⅜	2	Primary	
Long Rails	2	32¾	2½	⅞	Primary	
Short Rails	2	16¾	2½	⅞	Primary	
Long Cleats	2	29	1¼	⅞	Secondary	
Short Cleat	1	13	1¼	⅞	Secondary	
Cauls	7	21	3½	1⅝	Secondary	
Veneers	4	20	10			
Underlayment/Backer Veneer	3	18½	35		Straight grained	
Screws	8					#8 x 1¼ in.

Milling wood for this project is a little different from other projects because you're working mostly with veneer rather than with solid lumber. Because the core of the veneered top starts as rough stock, it should be taken through the rough and finish mill processes, which are described in more detail on p. 7.

TOOL LIST

POWER TOOLS
Bandsaw
Jointer
Tablesaw
Thickness planer

HAND TOOLS
Bench plane
Combination square
Straightedge
Veneer saw or
   utility knife

DESIGN Options

THE METAL BASE of this table adds a lot to the overall design, but you can also make something out of wood. This base is made from mahogany and has simple tapered legs and rails. You can still do the same veneer work for the top, but to complete the table, an edge-band needs to be added to all four sides of the core. Try using thin strips of the same material for the base. Alternatively, you could veneer the edges, which would be a bit more challenging but also more dramatic.

Making the core

The top starts as 2-in.-thick pieces of white pine that's 6 in. wide. It's best not to glue veneer to flatsawn material like this (**photo 1**) because the wood expands and contracts mostly across the grain, and the movement over a top this wide most likely would crack the veneer over time. The first step is to mill this wood into quartersawn pieces with the grain running perpendicular to the face of the board (**photo 2**) and then to glue them back together.

Glue up the planks. Glue three pieces of pine, each 2 in. thick, 6 in. wide, and about 3 ft. long, together face to face. Be sure to give the glue at least 24 hours to dry.

Lay out the cuts. This thick piece of material will be sliced into lengthwise strips, each about 1⅛ in. thick. Mark the cuts along both edges of the blank with a combination square (**photo 3**).

Cut the strips. Make sure the bandsaw is fitted with a fairly wide blade (the one I used is ⅝ in.) and that the tension is adjusted properly. Cut out the two outermost strips, one from each side of the blank. Take your time and don't rush (**photo 4**).

Re-mark and recut. Mark the next pair of strips, one from each side of what's left, with the combination square and a straightedge and make those cuts (**photo 5**).

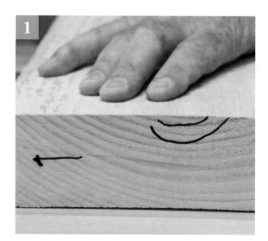

T-Mac Tip

The cuts don't have to be perfect because the pieces will be flattened and planed again. But if the cuts are really ragged, you can run both faces of the blank over the jointer before cutting the second pair of slices.

Remill the pieces. Treat these four pieces of material just as you would rough stock: flatten one face on the jointer, then joint one edge, run the pieces through the thickness planer (**photo 6**), and make the two edges parallel on the tablesaw by ripping them to width. The pieces should be 1 in. thick.

Glue up the core. You now have four boards, which together will be wide enough to make the core. Spread glue over the adjoining edges and clamp them together (**photo 7**). Always start by applying pressure to the middle clamp first, and then work your way out toward each end. You should be able to see glue squeeze-out along the full length of all the joints (**photo 8**). When the glue has dried, clean the surfaces.

T-Mac Tip

If there are knots or other blemishes on the edges of some of the boards, put them toward the outside. Because the top still needs to be trimmed to size, you may be able to cut away the imperfections.

Prepping the core

Wet it down. When the veneer arrives, it's going to be very brittle (**photo 1**) and difficult to work with. The first step is to prepare the veneer by spraying veneer softener on both sides of each piece of veneer (**photo 2**). After spraying both sides of each piece, make a stack of alternating layers of veneer and newspaper on a piece of ¾-in. plywood

Let the veneer dry. When the stack is complete, make a rudimentary veneer press by placing another piece of plywood on top and weighting it down, or clamping it, so the sheets of veneer are flat. Periodically, replace damp newspaper with dry sheets and continue this process until the veneer and the newspaper are dry. This process could take a day or two. When the veneer comes out of the press, it is very flexible and will be stable and ready for use (**photo 3**).

Rough-cut the core. Clean up both surfaces of the core, then trim the edges to make them parallel and trim the ends to make them perpendicular to the edges. Leave the core about 1 in. longer

and about ½ in. wider than its finished dimensions **(photo 4)**.

Cut the backer veneer. To minimize wood movement, two layers of veneer are glued to each side of the core. The first is a backer piece of mahogany, with the grain running perpendicular to that of the core. Lay out the backer veneer and cut pieces slightly oversize with a utility knife or a veneer saw **(photo 5)**.

Tape the pieces together. It will take more than one piece of backer veneer to completely cover the face of the core. After cutting as many sheets as you'll need, true up two adjoining edges with a straightedge and knife **(photo 6)** or veneer saw and tape the pieces together with veneer tape **(photo 7)**.

T-Mac Tip

If you have a lot of veneer to process, you can stack pieces together between two boards with ⅛ in. exposed, clamp the boards together, and run the whole stack over a jointer.

Gluing Down Veneer

The key to gluing veneer to a substrate is using the right amount of glue and then applying even pressure over the entire surface.

Glue can be spread with a roller or a glue dispenser **(photo 1).** Although yellow glue will work, cold press glue has a longer open time, and its consistency makes it easy to spread. Apply an even coat that completely covers the surface, but don't use too much. If you do, it will bleed through the pores of the veneer.

The core is clamped between two double layers of medium-density fiberboard (MDF) or plywood. Cauls placed across the width of the core every 4 in. to 5 in. exert even pressure.

To get enough clamping pressure in the middle of the stack where the clamps can't reach, you could cut curved cauls. But here's another trick: Rip one strip of wood at $1/16$ in. and two strips at $1/32$ in. Glue the strips to one of the pieces of MDF or plywood with the thin strips running lengthwise 4 in. from each edge and then place the thicker one in the middle.

Now the layers can be assembled. Start with two thicknesses of MDF or plywood, followed by a layer of backer

veneer, the core (freshly coated with glue), a second piece of backer, and, finally, the top layers of MDF or plywood. Put the MDF with the strips glued to it on the very top of the pile **(photo 2).**

Place the cauls across the top of the stack **(photo 3)** and clamp the assembly together, exerting good pressure. Start clamping in the middle and work your way toward each end **(photo 4).**

Let the stack dry for a day before removing the clamps. You may add cauls on the bottom of the stack as well. Add a layer of wax paper between the veneer and the plywood to prevent glue bleed-through.

T-Mac Tip

After all of the clamps have been tightened, those in the middle will have loosened up because the stack has been compressed. Go back and recheck all of the clamps and retighten those that need it.

Visiting a Metal Fabricator

The base of this table is made from pieces of mild steel formed in graceful curves, welded together, and then powder-coated a deep black. Steel offers a lot of design possibilities that wood doesn't, but working with it takes more than standard woodworking equipment, so I turned to Payne Engineering for help.

Working from sketches I provided, the first steps in the fabrication began with cutting all the leg pieces to length. Each curved piece has a small, flat section at the top end, which is formed on a press. Then a rolling machine makes the gentle arc.

Once the pieces are formed, they are welded together, a process that takes a couple of hours. The welds are ground down to make them smooth.

Once formed, the pieces are welded together.

When the welding is complete, the base is then sent out for powder-coating, a process in which powder is bound electrostatically to metal before the piece is heated in an oven to melt the powder into a smooth, hard coating.

Above top: Lengths of steel for the table base are cut to length.

Above center: A press forms a small flat section on the ends of the curved pieces.

Above bottom: A rolling machine creates the gentle arc in the side pieces.

Welds are ground smooth before the assembled base is powder-coated.

Cutting the face veneer

Use pieces from the same flitch.
The top is made from four pieces of burl veneer from the same flitch, meaning the sheets are in sequential order. That ensures that the color and grain pattern will be very close from one sheet of veneer to the next (**photo 1**).

Visualize the pattern. One way of visualizing what the top will look like is to tape two mirrors together along one edge, so they can be opened and closed like a book, and place them on a sheet of veneer (**photo 2**).

With the mirrors forming a 90-degree angle, you can see what a four-piece top would look like. By changing the angle of the mirrors, you can get an entirely different look (**photo 3**). This allows you see what you're going to get before you cut any of this expensive material.

Trace the edges. In looking at the pattern of the grain in the veneer, I realized I could create a diamond shape in the middle of the top by arranging four sheets of veneer. I stacked four pieces together and arranged the mirrors on top of the pile, then traced both inside edges of the mirror on the stack (**photo 4**).

Cut the pieces. Using a veneer saw or knife, cut along the layout line on the top sheet (**photo 5**). Take the next sheet in the flitch, flip it over, and align the edges so the grain pattern matches (**photo 6**). Draw a line on the second sheet (**photo 7**) and cut that edge. Cut the third and fourth pieces in the same way, shooting the edges with a plane if they don't align perfectly.

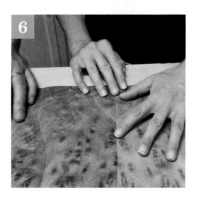

Tape the pieces together. With the face side of two of the pieces up, use a few pieces of masking tape to hold the veneer together. Then flip the pieces over and tape the back side of the veneer with more masking tape to hold those pieces together tightly **(photo 8).** Flip the pieces over once more and apply veneer tape to the face **(photo 9).** Now the masking tape on the back of the veneer can be removed (don't forget to do this!).

Repeat on the other half. The two pieces of veneer taped together are one-half of the pattern. Repeat the previous steps to form the other half of the pattern.

Marry the two halves. With a square aligned along the centerline of one piece, use a straightedge to cut a clean edge **(photo 10).** Repeat on the other half along the edges so the grain matches, then tape the pieces together. The veneer is now ready to be glued to the core **(photo 11)**. When you glue everything together, make sure to use a second piece of backer veneer on the bottom of the core so each side has two layers of veneer.

Finishing up

When the core comes out of the clamps, it will still need trimming to bring it to its finished dimension, and the veneer tape will have to be removed **(photo 1)**.

Trim the top. Lay out the final dimensions from the seams in the pattern. Bandsaw just outside the layout line on one edge, then clean up that edge on a jointer. Using the jointed edge as a reference, rip and crosscut the other sides to their finished dimensions **(photo 2)**.

Finish and install. For the finish, I applied a coat of linseed oil to both sides of the top, let the oil dry, and then applied several coats of lacquer. Whatever you use, just remember to finish the bottom just as you do the top so it won't warp.

The finished top just drops into the metal frame of the base and is held in place with a couple of screws **(photo 3)**.

LAMINATED COAT RACK

Stack Laminations from Precise Milling

This coat rack gets its dramatic geometric pattern from the same techniques used to make decorative banding found on furniture, only on a much larger scale.

Although the finished project looks complex, the method for creating it is straightforward. Plus, it allows a great deal of design flexibility. Alternating pieces of maple and cherry are glued together to create planks, then formed into a log and cut into strips. The strips are arranged into a diagonal pattern and then glued around a solid core.

The key to this project is precise milling. Many pieces must be glued together to form the various components, which must be uniform in size if you want a good result. In

addition to carefully following the basics of rough and finish milling, shop tools must be correctly adjusted.

The post for the coat rack is the centerpiece of the design. Although I've used cherry and maple to get alternating dark and light colors, you could just as easily use other woods and vary the pattern to get something that is more pleasing to your eye.

On a much smaller scale, the same techniques used to make the post and base can be used to make your own decorative inlays for other pieces of furniture. Although the pieces are a tiny fraction of the size of the coat rack parts, the basic approach is exactly the same.

Coat Rack

Post Detail

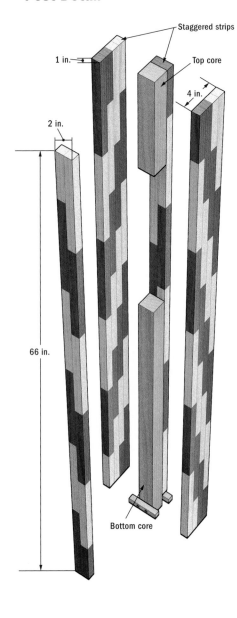

- Staggered strips
- 1 in.
- 2 in.
- 66 in.
- Top core
- 4 in.
- Bottom core

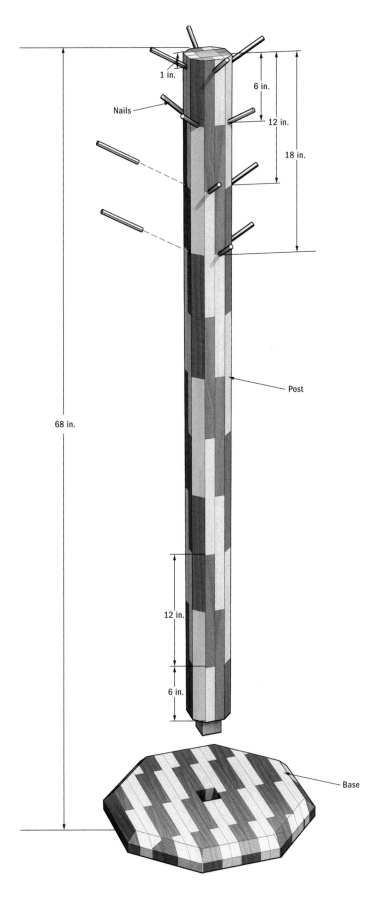

- 1 in.
- Nails
- 6 in.
- 12 in.
- 18 in.
- 68 in.
- Post
- 12 in.
- 6 in.
- Base

MATERIALS LIST/ROUGH MILL

PART	# OF PIECES	LENGTH (IN.)	WIDTH (IN.)	THICKNESS (IN.)	NOTES
Wood 1	2	38	7	$1\frac{1}{8}$	
Wood 2	2	38	7	$1\frac{1}{8}$	
Bottom Core	1	37	$2\frac{1}{2}$	$2\frac{1}{8}$	
Top Core	1	13	$2\frac{1}{2}$	$2\frac{1}{8}$	
Cleats	1	10	$\frac{7}{8}$	$\frac{7}{8}$	
Base	2	21	7	$2\frac{1}{8}$	
Nails	16				6-in. galvanized
Screws	12				#8 x $1\frac{1}{2}$-in. wood screws
Screws	3				#6 x $\frac{3}{4}$-in. wood screws

TOOL LIST

POWER TOOLS
Bandsaw
Cordless drill
Jointer
Router
Tablesaw
Thickness planer

HAND TOOLS
Bench chisels
Combination square
Handplane
Mallet

Tenon Detail

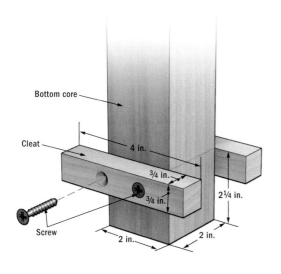

Bottom core

Cleat

Screw

4 in.

3/4 in.

3/4 in.

2 in.

2 in.

2¼ in.

DESIGN Options

ONE OF OUR DESIGN options was swapping out the patterned base for one made out of solid cherry. There are many possibilities. I strongly encourage you to have fun and tailor the design in a way that will make it your own.

Milling Rough Stock

Most furniture projects require that rough stock be milled into finished lumber with smooth, parallel faces and parallel edges. Careful milling here is even more important because so many individual pieces are glued together.

First, flatten one face on the jointer. Make sure the outfeed table is in line with the cutter head, that both tables are flat, and that the fence is 90 degrees to the bed. Check grain direction carefully **(photo 1)** and orient the stock so the cutter head won't run against the grain and potentially cause tearout.

Grain direction often changes, so you may have to take a couple of passes to decide which way is the best compromise.

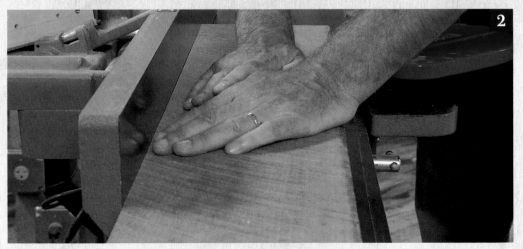

On the jointer, hand placement is critical. As soon as 6 in. to 8 in. of stock has cleared the cutter head, transfer your weight to the outfeed table **(photo 2).** Never, and I mean never, use the heel of your hand to push the back of the board over the cutter head.

Once you've flattened one face, joint one edge.

When you run the material through the thickness planer, remember that the cutter head is on the top, so the grain direction should be opposite of what you chose for the jointer. Take light passes.

With the two faces flat and parallel, put the jointed edge of the board against the tablesaw fence and cut off the rough edge. Make sure the blade is 90 degrees to the table **(photo 3)** and that the fence is parallel to the blade. Use a push stick whenever the distance between the blade and the fence is less than the width of your hand **(photo 4).**

Make sure the tablesaw has a splitter so that stock under tension can't pinch the blade and cause kickback. Finally, never use your left hand to pull the offcut

away from the blade, because if the stock kicks back, it could drag your hand into the blade. It's advisable to keep your left hand planted firmly on the table, out of the way, and use your right hand to hold the push stick **(photo 5).**

Blending Art and Function

Above top: A sketch is created from the inspiration.

Above bottom: Templates are made next.

Above top: Shaping the shoots.

Above bottom: The shoots glued together.

In his Long Island, New York, studio, David Ebner proves that something practical can also be a work of art.

Case in point is his "Scallion Coat Rack," a sculpture nearly 6 ft. high that started as a sketch of plants growing in a field next to his studio.

Turning that sketch into an object of human scale starts with shop drawings and then templates of the top of the plant. Two of the four shoots were cut out of solid ash, while the other two, because of their sharp bends, were made from ash laminations that wouldn't break if the coat rack were to be tipped over.

Working with a spokeshave, files, a card scraper, and finally sandpaper, Ebner brings each piece to its final shape and then glues them together.

To form the bulb of the plant, Ebner adds blocks on two sides of the base and then progressively builds it up with smaller slabs of ash on each side. He mounts the piece on a lathe for final shaping.

Once the bulb has been formed and sanded, it's time for finish. After bleaching and lightly sanding, Ebner adds paint.

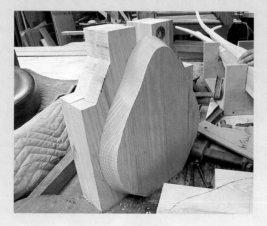

The base, formed from multiple pieces of solid wood.

Above top: The glued-up blank mounted on a lathe.

Above bottom: Finishing the piece with paint.

Cutting and reassembling

Start with four pieces of stock, each 38 in. long, 1 in. thick, and 7 in. wide, two of maple and two of cherry. Cut each board into three 12-in. pieces. To ensure they're all exactly the same length, use a tablesaw boat with a stop block clamped to the fence (**photo 1**). Your first cut should be to square up the end of the board (**photo 2**).

Glue pieces end to end. When you're finished you'll have six pieces of maple and six pieces of cherry, each exactly 12 in. long. Take one of each and glue them together end to end (**photo 3**). End-grain glue joints don't have much strength, but we don't need a super bond here. Make sure the edges as well as the faces are flush.

Make a longer board. Glue together a second and then a third pair of boards and then glue two of those pairs together with a longer set of clamps (**photo 4**). To join the last pair, you may not have a pair of clamps long enough. If that's the case, glue blocks to the edges of the last parts to be joined and use a smaller clamp (**photo 5**).

Clean up the glue. You now should have two 6-ft. planks of alternating pieces of maple and cherry (**photo 6**). Clean them up on the thickness planer by removing just enough material to flatten and true the surfaces.

Make the pattern. To create the step pattern, cut 6 in. from one end of one of the planks (**photo 7**). Then glue the two planks together, face to face, and allow the glue to dry overnight. Next, cut off the overhanging 6 in. on the end of the plank (**photo 8**) and run both edges of the board over the jointer to clean up any glue residue.

Cut into strips. At the tablesaw, cut the blank into strips 1 in. thick. You should have six of them.

Building the post

Make a tenon. The strips will be glued around a 2-in.-square core of scrap material (the core doesn't have to run the full length of the post). To create a tenon that will connect the post to the base, screw strips of scrap material to one end of the core 2 in. from the end (**photo 1**).

Arrange the strips. Lay the pieces flat on the bench (**photo 2**). Rotate every other board end for end, keeping the same face up (that's the first, third, and fifth boards). This creates an even more interesting pattern (**photo 3**). The surfaces facing up will be the ones that are glued to the core. Now, separate the strips into a single, a double, a single, and another double (**photo 4**) and edge-glue the two pairs of strips together.

Glue the first strips to the core. Flip the two narrow strips up on edge, rolling them so the upper face of each faces the core. Make sure the ends of the strips are snug against the index blocks that will create the tenon (**photo 5**). Glue the strips to the core.

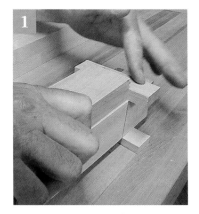

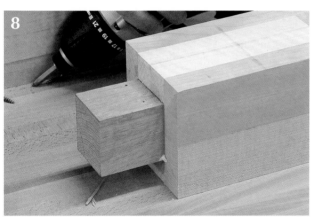

Glue on the wide pieces. The wide pieces can be glued to the core. Arrange the pieces to maintain the step pattern around the post **(photo 6)**. When the glue has dried, remove the index blocks **(photo 7)**. As you'll see, the index blocks have created clean, even shoulders all the way around the tenon **(photo 8)**.

Chamfer the edges. To lighten the look of the post, chamfer the corners on the tablesaw. Set the blade at 45 degrees, and set the fence so you're cutting away $3/4$ in. at each corner **(photo 9)**. Then run the post past the blade until all the corners have been cut.

Making the base

The pattern in the base is up to you. This one was made from the leftover scraps of the maple and cherry used to make the post. Whether you do it this way or make it from solid material, the technique is the same.

Make the blank. Start with a blank that's about $20^1/2$ in. square and a piece of plywood that's exactly 20 in. square **(photo 1)**. Find the center of both and screw them together right at the center point. At the bandsaw, cut just outside the plywood, then clean up the rough cuts you've made at the tablesaw using a L-fence to ride against the plywood.

Cut the corners. Using a combination square, spin the plywood until you've created an octagon **(photo 2).** Set a second screw through the plywood to hold it in position. Cut off the ears at the bandsaw and true up the cuts on the tablesaw, once again using the L-fence.

Cut the mortise. Lay out the mortise for the post at the center of the base. Hog out most of the waste with a drill **(photo 3),** and finish by paring to your layout lines with a chisel **(photo 4).**

Chamfer the edges. Using the tablesaw or a chamfering bit and router, cut a chamfer around the edges of the base.

Apply the finish of your choice. For this project we sprayed on a number of coats of lacquer, sanding between coats with 320-grit paper. Whatever finish you use, follow the manufacturer's instructions.

Insert the pegs. Although we tried several options, we ended up using stainless-steel dowels for the pegs. To ensure that all the holes were drilled at the same angle, we made a simple jig. It consisted of a block of wood with a hole bored in the middle, which was cut to the desired angle and attached to a strip of wood that could then be easily clamped to the post **(photo 5).**

CONSOLE TABLE

Making Curved Parts

The design for this console table was inspired by a bookshelf that Eli Cleveland made for a local library. The slender curves of the piece he built were incorporated into the overall look of this table.

Central to the design are three identical legs, each made of two opposing curves that are glued together at the center. Curved components have a long history in furniture making (see my Road Trip on p. 126), and there are at least two ways of making them. Steam-bending is one technique, but a simpler approach is bent lamination, described in detail in Build Your Skills on p. 124.

One of the most intriguing parts of this project is how the curved legs seem to grow right out of the shelf. Getting that effect takes some careful fitting, which can be time-consuming. But it's not as difficult as it might look, and the impact it makes on the overall design is worth the effort.

This table was made from walnut selected for its uniform color and grain pattern. It would make a beautiful addition in a hall, behind a sofa, or, as we intended, as a console that is positioned under a wall-mounted flat-screen television (see Design Options on p. 131).

Console Table

14 in.

39 in.

12 in.

5/8 in.

7/8 in.

33 in.

Top

7/8 in.

3/16 in.

Top batten

14 3/4 in.

10 in.

Shelf

Shelf batten

1 5/16 in.

1 5/16 in.

1 5/16 in.

5/8 in.

Leg (lamination)

1 5/16 in.

MATERIALS LIST/ROUGH MILL

PART	# OF PIECES	LENGTH (IN.)	WIDTH (IN.)	THICKNESS (IN.)	WOOD
Laminate/Caul	6	37	6½	1⁷⁄₁₆	Primary
Shelf Battens	4	11	1³⁄₈	³⁄₄	Primary
Top Battens	6	13	1³⁄₈	³⁄₄	Primary
Shelf	2	37	6½	⁷⁄₈	Primary
Top	1	40	14½	1¼	Primary
Plywood	1	36	24	³⁄₄	

Mill the stock to its rough dimensions and allow it to sit overnight separated by stickers. The following day, bring the pieces to their finished dimensions and clean up any millmarks with a handplane. This process is described in more detail on p. 7.

TOOL LIST

POWER TOOLS
Bandsaw
Cordless drill
Jointer
Tablesaw
Thickness planer

HAND TOOLS
Bench chisels
Bench plane
Combination
  square
Dead-blow hammer
Glue scraper
Miter gauge
Straightedge

Patterns

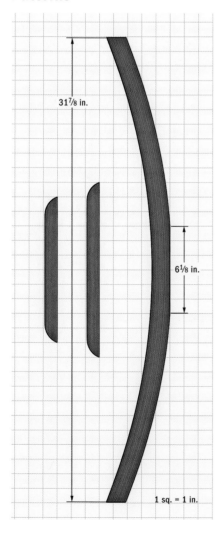

31⁷⁄₈ in.

6⅛ in.

1 sq. = 1 in.

Making the bending form

To build the form for the legs, cut a piece of ³⁄₄-in. plywood to 33 in. by 6½ in. Mark 1 in. in from each end, and square the mark 2 in. from the edge. At the center, mark 5¼ in. from the edge. Draw a curve through these points and extend the curve to the board's end. Cut out the curve and fair it to remove bumps. Keep the edges square.

Screw the pattern to another piece of plywood, bandsaw the new piece close to the pattern, and flush-cut the second piece to the first. Screw the curves to a base.

Drill 1½-in.-deep by 1½-in.-diameter holes 2 in. from the curved edge, for C-clamps during glue-up. You can also build the form with two parallel faces, which works better with hand screws (**photo 1**).

Making Curved Parts from Straight Stock

The curved legs are central to the design of the table, and once you understand the bent lamination technique, it can be applied to many different types of furniture.

The process amounts to cutting a solid piece of stock into a number of pliable strips that can be bent around a form **(photo 1).** Just how thin to make the plies depends on how sharp the bend will be: A tighter curve requires thinner material so it won't crack. Because the legs of this table follow a gentle curve, the plies are about ⅛ in. thick.

Once the rough stock has been milled to 37 in. long, 6 in. wide, and 1⁷⁄₁₆ in. thick, mark a chevron (an indicating arrow) on one face **(photo 2).** This allows you to keep all the plies in the same order in which they were cut, which will ensure that the laminated part looks as if it were made from a single piece of wood.

Cut the strips on the tablesaw **(photo 3).** You'll need a total of 66 strips—11 for each of the six legs. Save the last offcut for use as a caul during glue-up.

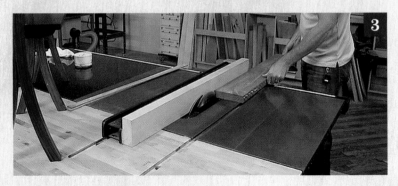

T-Mac Tip

Apply a thin coat of wax to the table and your rip fence before tackling all those cuts. It will make the work go smoothly.

By cutting ⅛-in.-thick plies with a blade that's ⅛ in. thick, you're losing half your material in sawdust. It may be tempting to switch to a thin-kerf blade, but these blades have a tendency to heat up when cutting thick material and as a result will wobble slightly. That makes for a rougher cut, so you're better off sticking with a standard blade. Worth noting: It also depends on the quality of the thin-kerf blade.

Lay out the 11 plies for one leg on the bench in the same order in which they were cut, using the chevron as your guide **(photo 4).** Spread glue on the faces of the plies **(photo 5)**, but hold out the last ply—you don't want glue on the outer face of that one.

Now the plies can be reassembled, once again in the same order **(photo 6),** and clamped to the form **(photo 7).** Use the caul you saved from ripping the strips on the outside of the leg to help distribute the clamping pressure evenly. To ensure the glue squeeze-out doesn't bond the leg to the form, apply some wax to the form first.

When you clamp the plies, make sure to start in the middle and work your way out toward the ends. When you've set your last clamp, go back and make sure they're all tight. The clamps you put on first probably will have loosened up.

At this point, the plies are still a little long. If those on the ends don't close up tightly from clamping pressure alone, you can sink a single screw at the end to hold everything together.

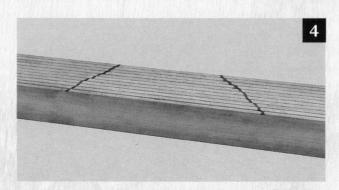

Curved Furniture with a Pedigree

Thonet's 19th-century bent-wood rocker could be knocked down into components to make shipping easier.

Thonet's designs ranged from doll furniture to easels.

A German-Austrian cabinetmaker named Michael Thonet developed a radically different kind of furniture in the 1830s by laminating and ultimately steam-bending parts into graceful curves. One of the most famous chairs of all time, Thonet's "Chair no. 14," has been reproduced millions of times.

On our *Rough Cut* Road Trip we visited the Brooklyn Museum in New York, which houses a collection of Thonet's work. The collection includes a rocker that could be knocked down into flat components to make shipping easier. Dozens could fit into a crate and then be reassembled.

While chairs of all types were his mainstay, he also diversified his products to an extent that hadn't been seen before.

This included everything from furniture for dolls to an adjustable bent-wood easel.

Thonet's work has had a lasting impact on furniture design. A chair designed by famed American architect Frank Gehry, for instance, is all about bent lamination. Gehry's design is thoroughly modern, but it has its roots in the 19th-century work of Thonet and his family.

Top and bottom: Bent-laminated work by Frank Gehry.

Finishing the legs

Allow the legs to dry at least overnight. Before removing the assembly from the form, mark the leg at the centerline of the form (**photo 1**). This will allow you to align two legs later when it comes time to glue them together. Now, pop the leg out of the form. If the leg seems stuck, a tap with a dead-blow hammer should do the trick.

Clean up the glue. Remove the glue residue from the edge of the leg with a glue scraper (**photo 2**). Make one pass on the jointer and send the legs through the thickness planer to bring them to their final thickness of $1^5/_{16}$ in.

Mill the flats. At the tablesaw, align the centerline of the leg with the centerline on the jig (**photo 3**), then clamp the leg securely to the form. Adjust the rip fence so it allows you to remove $^1/_{16}$ in. of material from the outer face of the leg (if you remove a little bit of the form in making the cut, that's OK). Then run the form and leg through the saw. Mill all six legs at this fence setting (**photo 4**). You're aiming for a flat spot that is about $6^1/_8$ in. long.

Re-mark the leg. Before removing the leg from the form, transfer the center-line from the jig back to the leg (**photo 5**). Next, transfer the length marks from the jig to both ends of the leg (**photo 6**).

Cut the legs to length. At the bandsaw, cut the legs to length at the marks you've just drawn (**photo 7**).

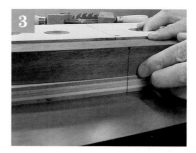

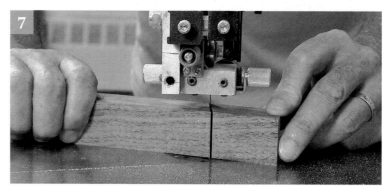

Assembling the legs

Glue up the legs. Glue two legs together, flat to flat, with the centerlines aligned with each other (**photo 1**). Check the diagonals (**photo 2**) and make sure the measurements are the same, even if you have to shift the centerlines slightly. Then allow the glue to set for a couple of hours. Repeat this process for the other two pairs of legs.

Lay out the rabbets and dadoes. Each leg assembly gets a dado at the center and rabbets at each end for the battens that will support the top and center shelf. Mark the rabbets on the ends of the legs, $7/8$ in. wide and $3/16$ in. deep (**photo 3**). To lay out the dado at the center of the leg, lay a straightedge across the tops of the legs and measure down $14^3/4$ in. for the start of the dado (**photo 4**). The dado is $7/8$ in. wide and $3/16$ in. deep. The outer legs are dadoed only on the inside face. The center leg gets the dado on both faces. Lay out rabbets on the tops of all the legs, inside and out.

Cut the dadoes. Set up a $7/8$-in. stack dado at the tablesaw with the depth of cut set at $3/16$ in. To give the leg more stability as it's run over the stack dado, screw a scrap of plywood across the end (**photo 5**). Then cut all the dadoes at their marked locations (**photo 6**). For the center leg, cut the dado on one face, flip it over, remove the plywood, and attach it to the other side to make the second cut.

Cut the rabbets. Attach a sacrificial fence to the rip fence and move it over until it just touches the dado. Then run the legs over the dado (**photo 7**). Both sides of each leg assembly should be rabbeted. Take your time and don't rush it. Clean up any millmarks from the faces of the legs with a handplane.

Make the battens. Cut out four 10-in. battens for the center shelf and six 12-in. battens for the top. They are $^7/8$ in. wide and $^5/8$ in. thick. If you like, gently round the ends for a softer look. A tight fit is important, so mill the battens so they're just slightly oversize and use a handplane to trim for a perfect fit (**photo 8**). To help you get the battens centered on the legs, mark a centerline on each (**photo 9**).

Glue in the battens. Glue the battens into their respective dadoes and rabbets (**photo 10**). To minimize squeeze-out, don't use too much glue.

Making the shelf

The shelf is made from two boards that are 36 in. long and 5¾ in. wide. The pieces are notched and fitted to the legs and glued together in place. This notching is what makes it look as if the center leg grows out from the shelf.

Mark the notches. At the ends of the shelf pieces, mark notches that are ⁵⁄₈ in. deep and a total of 1⁵⁄₁₆ in. wide (**photo 1**). At the center, mark a notch that's 1⁵⁄₁₆ in. wide and 1⁵⁄₁₆ in. long in each direction (**photo 2**).

Cut out the notches. At the tablesaw, use a boat or miter gauge to cut the notches. Set the blade height at 1⁵⁄₁₆ in. and use a stop block to align the work correctly to the blade (**photo 3**). After cutting the edges of the notches on the tablesaw, take out the rest of the material on the bandsaw and clean up the cuts with a bench chisel.

Fit the shelf. Fit each half of the shelf around the legs (**photo 4**). This process can be frustrating, so take your time and aim for a good fit. The two edges of the boards should come together at the same time the notches snug up to the legs. When the fit is right, apply glue to the edges of the shelf pieces and clamp them together around the legs (**photo 5**). Add the end leg assemblies for stability.

Check for square. Measure the distance between the tops of the legs on the top and the bottom and adjust the clamps until the measurements are the same.

Attach the shelf and top. With the table upside down on the bench, drive screws through pilot holes at the end of the battens into the shelf (**photo 6**), then attach the top. Make sure the overhang of the top is even on the ends and the sides.

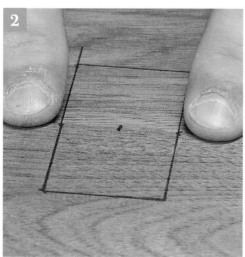

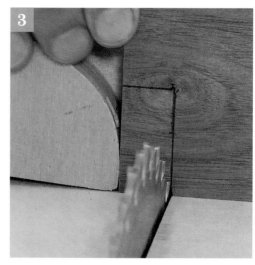

Finishing up

Once all surfaces have been thoroughly cleaned and sanded with 150- or 220-grit sandpaper, apply the finish of your choice. For this project, we applied a coat of linseed oil to bring out the color of the walnut, then allowed it to dry (which can take up to a week). We finished with several coats of shellac.

DESIGN Options

THIS TABLE WOULD be perfect for holding a DVD player and other components for a television. But if I were to use the table in a hall or behind a couch, I'd probably change the curve of the legs to widen its stance and make it a little less tippy; I'd also lighten up the look of the entire piece by making all of the parts a little thinner and more delicate. The look of the table can also be changed dramatically depending on the species of wood you're using. Tiger maple would create a completely different appearance.

SAND-SHADED CLOCK

Shading Veneer

This veneered clock face is flat, but it looks three-dimensional because of the shading along the edges. The three-dimensional look is further enhanced by the addition of the scalloped edges made from black veneer.

The shading is done with hot sand, exactly as it was more than 200 years ago in the shops of New England's finest craftsmen. Work of the Federal period includes many examples of decorative inlays that were made this way (see my Road Trip to The Metropolitan Museum of Art on p. 136).

Veneer comes in many varieties, so you can easily customize this design. In this project, we've used two kinds of veneer, holly and black costello, both of which are readily available.

The veneered pattern takes the place of numbers on a conventional clock face. Each segment is one-twelfth of the face, so it represents one hour.

The face is easy to lay out with nothing more than a compass and a straightedge. The curved shadows around the outside of the face are made with a simple plywood template.

In terms of materials, you won't need much—just a couple of pieces of $\frac{1}{2}$-in.-thick plywood, roughly 5 sq. ft. of straight-grained light veneer, and about 1 sq. ft. of dark veneer for the shadows at the perimeter of the face. A battery-operated clock mechanism slips into a recess cut in the back of the face.

Sand-Shaded Clock

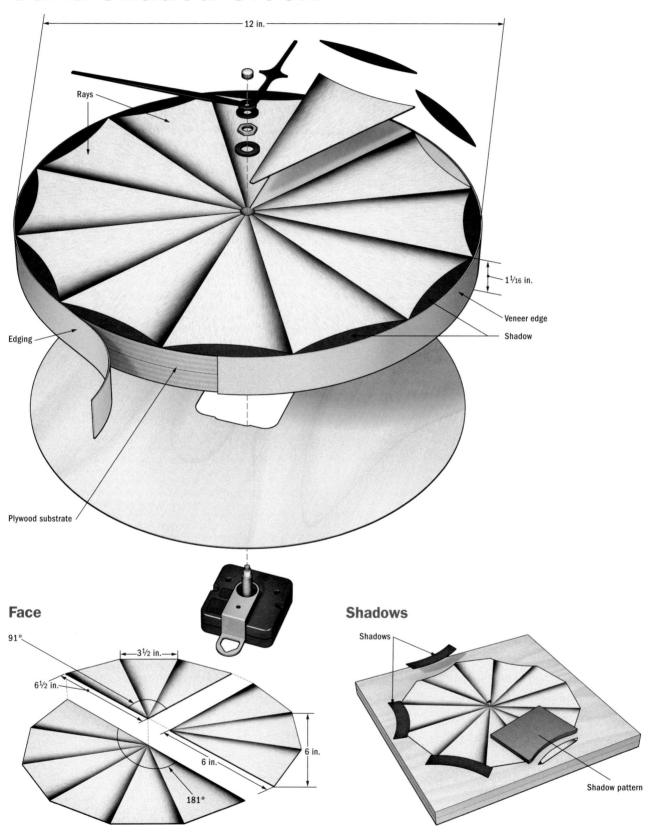

12 in.

Rays

1 1/16 in.

Veneer edge

Shadow

Edging

Plywood substrate

Face

91°

3 1/2 in.

6 1/2 in.

6 in.

6 in.

181°

Shadows

Shadows

Shadow pattern

MATERIALS LIST/ROUGH MILL

PART	# OF PIECES	LENGTH (IN.)	WIDTH (IN.)	THICKNESS (IN.)	NOTES
Plywood	5	15	15	½	
Light Veneer (Rays)	1				5 sq. ft. of straight-grained veneer
Dark Veneer	1				1 sq. ft. of black-dyed veneer
Medium-Density Fiberboard (MDF)	1	15	15	½	
Pan and Heating Element	1				Any metal pan and burner
Sand					5 cups, fine-grained, clean sand
Clock Mechanism	1				Battery operated

TOOL LIST

POWER TOOLS
Bandsaw
Cordless drill
Lathe
Router table

HAND TOOLS
Bench plane
Card scraper
Chisel
Combination square
Compass
Straightedge
Veneer tape

Prepping the materials

Plywood makes a good substrate because it's both stable and cheap. The veneered face of this clock is laid up over a core of birch plywood that's 1 in. thick.

Glue the plywood together. The first step is to cut two pieces of ½-in. plywood 15 in. square and glue them together face to face (**photo 1**). Let the glue dry overnight.

Treat the veneer. When the veneer gets to your shop, it's probably going to be too brittle to use. After cutting the veneer into manageable pieces, spray both sides of each piece with veneer softener (**photo 2**) and layer them between pieces of paper (**photo 3**).

Clamp the veneer and paper. Use a piece of plywood on either side of the veneer and paper. Change the paper as it absorbs water from the glue (every 12 hours or so) and let the veneer dry for a couple of days. When it comes out of the press, it will be pliable and easy to work with.

Inspired by History

Detailing on an early 19th-century sideboard by John and Thomas Seymour.

This clock face gets its distinctive, three-dimensional look from a technique called sand shading, and there's no better place to see how sand-shaded inlays can be used to decorate furniture than at the American Wing at the Metropolitan Museum of Art in New York City.

One of the prides of the museum's collection is a stunning sideboard made by a father-and-son team, John and Thomas Seymour, in Boston, Massachusetts, between 1807 and 1810.

The Seymours used a combination of light and dark veneers to lighten the look of this piece. A signature characteristic

The Seymour sideboard was made in Boston between 1807 and 1810.

of their work is the demilune inlay made with sand-shaded pieces of veneer. The Seymours also used this lunette banding in a beautiful tall clock that's also part of the museum's impressive collection.

The same techniques were being used by Philadelphia craftsmen of the same era. Also in the collection is a gentleman's secretary-bookcase that features 32 circular inlays, which have shading that helps give a hollowed or scooped-out look (at left).

The Seymours used lunette banding in a tall clock.

Sand shading gives circular inlays on a secretary-bookcase a three-dimensional look.

Laying out the face

Start with a circle. On a piece of poster board, draw a 12-in.-dia. circle. Without changing the setting of the compass, walk around the outside edge to divide the circle into six even segments **(photo 1).**

    Divide the segments. Set the compass to about half its previous setting (it doesn't have to be exact) and strike two intersecting arcs to find the center point between two adjacent one-sixth marks **(photos 2 and 3).** With a straightedge between the center of the circle and this intersection, divide the segment into two equal halves **(photo 4).** Set the compass to this distance and walk your way around the circle to divide it into 12 equal parts.

    Cut out one of the triangular pieces to use as a template for the veneer.

Cutting out the veneer

Cut the segments. Using your poster board pattern, trace the outline on a piece of the holly veneer (**photo 1**). The veneer may have some knots in it, and whether you include them or not is a matter of personal preference (**photo 2**). If you like them, have fun incorporating them into your design.

Lay out as many pieces as you can on a piece of veneer. Then with a very sharp knife and straightedge, cut them out (**photo 3**). Leave the pieces slightly oversize, and don't try to muscle your way through the veneer with a single pass.

Take your time and make several passes with the knife until each piece separates cleanly. You'll need a minimum of 12 pieces, but you should cut several extras.

Make a shooting board. To ensure a tight joint between pieces, you'll need to shoot the edges with a handplane. The easiest way to do that is with a simple shooting board. Our shooting board was made from pieces of MDF—one about 12 in. by 5 in. screwed to a slightly larger base and an arm about ³/₄ in. wide and 7 in. long (**photo 4**). The arm pivots on a piece of dowel, but if you have none on hand, you can also use a pencil stub.

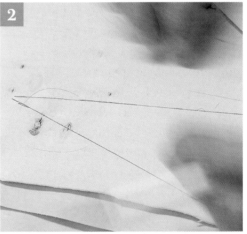

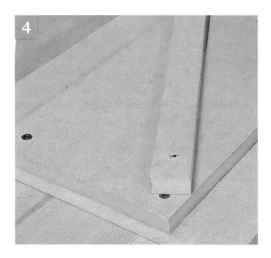

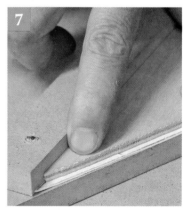

Shoot the edges. Place a piece of veneer on the shooting board and adjust the arm until one edge aligns with the arm and the other with the side of the base **(photo 5)**, then clamp the arm in position **(photo 6)**. The idea is to make the angle just a bit over 30 degrees, giving you a little extra material to work with as you complete the circle of the face.

Cut a piece of ¼-in. plywood to the same shape as your poster board pattern and use it to hold down the veneer as you plane the edge **(photo 7)**. Run the plane carefully over the edge until it's no longer removing material **(photo 8)**. Be sure to check that the edge is straight **(photo 9)**. Shoot both long edges of all the pieces.

Shading Veneer with Hot Sand

The pieces of veneer are given definition and depth by shading one edge. The shading technique involves a simple process of scorching the wood lightly in a pan of sand, the same technique used by Federal-era furniture makers in the 1800s **(photo 1).** The only difference is that I heated the sand with an electric hotplate.

Put about 1½ in. of sand into a metal pan. The type of sand isn't important—playground sand will work just fine—but you'll have to experiment with the temperature. If it's too hot or if you bury the edges too deeply, the veneer will burn, rendering it unusable **(photo 2).** Pay special attention to the tip of the veneer. Because it's thinner, it will burn more readily. It should take a couple of minutes to toast an edge. If it scorches in 30 seconds or so, your sand is way too hot.

You can save a little time by toasting several pieces at once **(photo 3).** Just keep an eye on them so they don't get really burned.

Once the pieces are done, shoot the edges again to remove any flaky material and straighten any distortions the veneer picked up from the heat **(photo 4).**

Assembling the face

Check the fit. Lay out the wedges in a circle, take each adjacent pair and fold them together face to face, and lightly shoot their common edges to make sure they will fit together without any gaps (**photo 1**).

Tape the edges. Use veneer tape to join four groups of three wedges each, paying close attention to the point where they meet. Get this as close as you can (**photo 2**). Each three-wedge piece should equal 90 degrees, which you can check with a combination square. If the angle is a little off (**photo 3**), take it to the shooting board and adjust it.

Completing the pattern. Once you've assembled the four quadrants, tape two of them together to form a half circle. Make a second half circle with the other pair and then tape both halves together with veneer tape (**photo 4**). Check edge alignment carefully as you go, and shoot any edges needed to achieve a tight fit.

Glue it down. Apply glue to the back of the veneer (the side without veneer tape) and to the plywood substrate (**photo 5**). Also apply glue to a piece of backer veneer for the back of the clock face, then assemble the layers between two ³/₄-in. plywood cauls. Clamp the assembly together and let it dry for a couple of hours. Once it comes out of the clamps, use dividers to draw a 12-in. circle from the center of the face. This is as good a time as any to remove your veneer tape. It can be a sticky situation. A nice trick is to use a spray bottle of water, allow 10 to 15 minutes for the adhesive to loosen, then peel it off by hand. If you run out of patience, use a card scraper.

T-Mac Tip

Use a piece of wax paper between the veneer and the cauls so the two won't stick together.

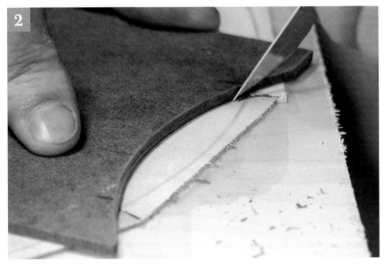

Creating the shadows

The perimeter of the face will be scalloped out to create 12 curved spaces, one at the end of each veneer wedge. These are the shadows that will be filled with black costello veneer.

Make curves. To start, make a curved pattern that's pleasing to your eye using ¼-in. plywood. Make the pattern big enough so it connects the points where each seam meets the circle (**photo 1**). (Note: You can use a tin can or a cup to shape the curve.) Cut along the edge of the pattern using a sharp knife (**photo 2**). Work your way around the face, but for now cut out only every other wedge.

T-Mac Tip

If your knife gets away from you and you slice into the veneer wedge, you can simply remove that wedge with a chisel and replace it with one of your spares.

Remove the waste. Clamp the face to the bench and use a sharp chisel to remove the waste (**photo 3**). Work carefully so you don't pry up any of the edges.

Cut the shadows. Use the same plywood pattern to cut out pieces of the black veneer and glue them onto the face using plywood cauls made from ¼-in. plywood (**photo 4**). Once every other shadow has been glued in, continue cutting and gluing the remaining six segments until the face is complete.

If the costello is thinner than the holly, you can double up the shadow pieces to get the surface flush.

When all of the shadow pieces have been glued in, the face will look something like the one in **photo 5,** and it can now be cut to its finished circular shape.

T-Mac Tip

If you cut the shadows at a slight angle, it will create a beveled edge. Place the thin edge up when you glue the shadow piece in place. That will make it easier to get tight seams.

Cutting out the face

Make a template. The face of the clock is beginning to emerge, but it needs to be turned from a square into a circle. Start by finding the center of a piece of plywood and drawing a 12-in. circle on one face. Cut out the circle on the bandsaw and then true it up by mounting it on a lathe **(photo 1).**

If you don't have a lathe, find another means to true the edges into a perfect circle. This is the template for the clock face, so you want it as clean and round as possible—even if it's a little less than 12 in. Drill a hole in the center of the plywood big enough for a screw to pass through, and countersink the hole. Drill a small hole at the center of the face using a drill press.

Bandsaw the circle. Start by screwing the template to the clock face, and bandsaw just outside the edge of the plywood **(photo 2).** Now reverse the template so it's on the bottom of the clock face and set a second screw along one of the diagonal lines so the template can't shift.

Complete the circle. Mount a bearing-guided bit in the router table **(photo 3)** and use it to remove the waste around the outside of the face. For safety's sake, mount a pivot on the router table and rest the work on that before easing it into the bit. As soon as the bit and bearing are fully engaged with the work, you can move the face away from the pivot and continue the cut **(photo 4).** Don't rush it.

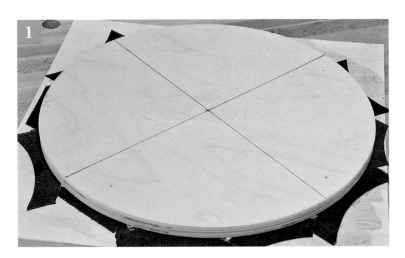

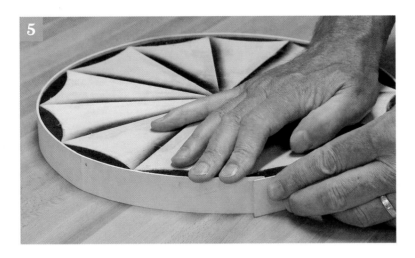

Add the banding. Cut a strip of veneer slightly longer than the circumference of the clock face. The ends of the strip should overhang each other slightly (**photo 5**). When the strip is glued on, leave an inch or so on each side of this overlap unglued. Later, cut through the pieces to make a clean, tight joint.

Apply glue to the back of the banding and wrap it around the clock face. Use a second piece of veneer as a caul and clamp everything together with plastic shrink wrap (**photo 6**).

Finishing up

Trim the banding. Once the glue has dried on the banding, trim the long edges where they overlap to make the joint tight and then glue and clamp the remaining veneer. Once dry, you want to finish it off by sanding all surfaces flush, being careful when removing any tape and glue on the face.

Finally, break the edges of the banding using 220-grit sandpaper. Take care in doing this because the banding edge is sharp and oversanding can damage the clock face.

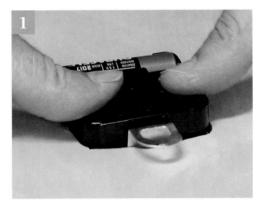

Install the hardware. Drill a hole through the center of the face large enough to accept the stem of the clock mechanism. Trace the outline of the mechanism on the back and rout out the space (**photo 1**). Then install the hardware.

Add the finish. For the finish, you can apply several coats of shellac and then wax. Whatever finish you use, follow the manufacturer's instructions for applying it.

SIMPLE BOOKCASE

Building a Router Jig

There's always a need for a well-constructed bookcase around the house. We've designed one that has three fixed and three adjustable shelves.

The fixed shelves, which fall at the top, bottom, and middle of the case, connect the two sides with through-mortise-and-tenon joinery. This type of joinery adds exceptional strength and beautiful detail when viewed from the side.

There are also two adjustable shelves above the middle fixed shelf and one below, but the placement of these shelves can be altered easily depending on your needs.

One of the standout features of this bookcase is the use of different species of wood. The sides and fixed shelves are made from dark walnut, while the back boards are made from lighter figured tiger maple and the adjustable shelves from light-colored hard maple. This use of contrasting woods, along with the natural imperfections like sapwood and knots, adds a lot of personality to the overall look and design of the piece. It also proves that you don't need to work with flawless boards to make a beautiful piece of furniture.

The top of the case has a stepped pattern, which was pleasing to my eye, but that's a detail that's easy to change (see "Design Options" on p. 157).

A key technique used in the construction of this bookcase is wedged through-mortise-and-tenon joinery. These joints are very strong, and you'll get plenty of practice perfecting them because you'll need a total of 18 to complete the project. Building a simple jig for the router is a big help (see Build Your Skills on p. 150 to learn how).

Simple Bookcase

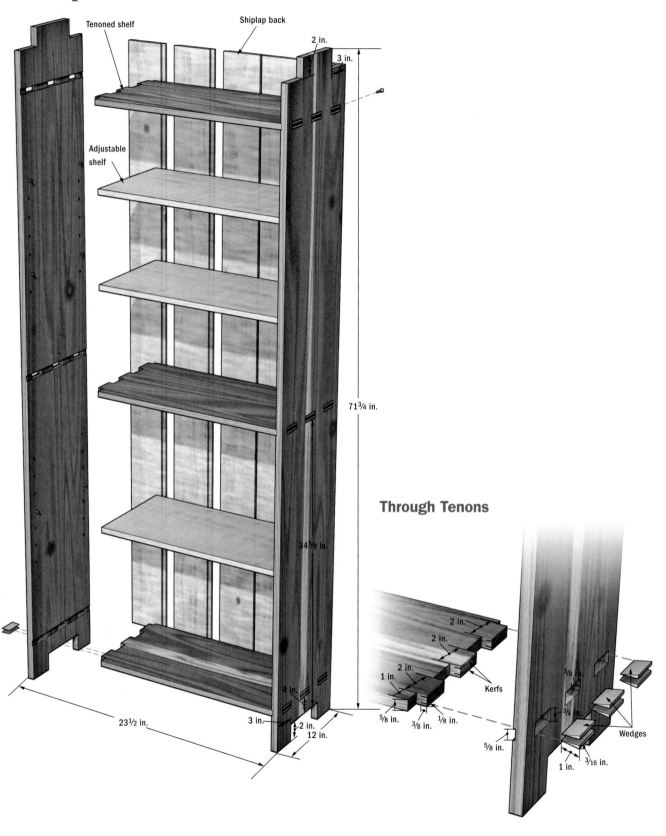

Tenoned shelf

Shiplap back

2 in.

3 in.

Adjustable shelf

71³/₄ in.

34⁵/₈ in.

Through Tenons

2 in.

2 in.

2 in.

1 in.

Kerfs

⁵/₈ in.

³/₈ in.

¹/₈ in.

4 in.

2 in.

12 in.

23¹/₂ in.

3 in.

³/₈ in.

³/₄ in.

⁵/₈ in.

1 in.

³/₁₆ in.

Wedges

MATERIALS LIST/ROUGH MILL

PART	# OF PIECES	LENGTH (IN.)	WIDTH (IN.)	THICKNESS (IN.)	WOOD	NOTES
Sides	2	$72\frac{3}{4}$	$12\frac{1}{2}$	$\frac{7}{8}$	Primary 1	
Tenoned Shelf	3	$24\frac{1}{2}$	$11\frac{15}{16}$	$\frac{3}{4}$	Primary 1	
Wedge	1	18	$7\frac{1}{2}$	$\frac{7}{8}$	Primary 2	
Adjustable Shelf	3	23	$11\frac{3}{4}$	$\frac{3}{4}$	Primary 2	
Shiplap Back (Inner)	3	$66\frac{3}{4}$	$5\frac{3}{8}$	$\frac{5}{8}$	Primary 2	
Shiplap Back (Ends)	2	$66\frac{3}{4}$	$5\frac{1}{8}$	$\frac{5}{8}$	Primary 2	
Adjustable Shelf Pins	12					$\frac{1}{4}$-in.-dia. shaft
Medium-Density Fiberboard(MDF)/ Plywood	1	24	24	$\frac{3}{4}$		
Screws	8					#8 x $1\frac{1}{4}$ in.
Screws	18					#8 x 1 in.

Getting materials ready for use is a two-step process. Start by rough-milling the stock and stickering it overnight. Then bring it to final dimensions the next day. For more information, see p. 7.

TOOL LIST

POWER TOOLS
Drill
Jointer
Router
Thickness planer
Tablesaw

HAND TOOLS
Bench chisels
Bench plane
Combination square
Dead-blow hammer
Mallet
Miter gauge
Utility knife

Back Detail

Making a Through-Mortise-and-Tenon Joint

Through-mortise-and-tenon joints are the central feature of this bookcase. They consist of tenons formed on the ends of the fixed shelves and mortises that are located in a shallow dado and cut all the way through the sides of the case.

The old-school way of making the mortises would be to define the sides of the dado with a knife, remove most of the waste with a shoulder plane, and then true up the dado with a router plane **(photo 1).** The more modern method of using a router is much faster.

To guide the router, build a simple jig that spans the width of each side piece **(photo 2).** The jig is made from four pieces of ¾-in.-thick, 3-in.-wide plywood. Two pieces are 12 in. long and two are 18 in. long.

To make the jig, place the two short pieces of plywood snugly against the side pieces and clamp them in place. Take one of the longer pieces and put it across the side. Use a combination square to make sure this crosspiece is square to the edge of the side piece **(photo 3),** then screw it to both of the short pieces.

Take the router you plan on using and place it against the first crosspiece. Place the second crosspiece against the base of the router to get the correct distance **(photo 4).** Next, make sure the two pieces are parallel, and then screw the second crosspiece in place. The router should slide smoothly but be held firmly on track.

Clamp the jig to a test piece and with a ⅝-in. bit set to a depth of ⅛ in., run a dado through both side pieces to create reference notches on both sides of the jig.

Making the dadoes

Lay out the shelf locations. After all the stock has been milled to finished dimensions and all millmarks removed with a handplane, lay out the location of the fixed shelves on each side piece. The first shelf sits 4 in. off the floor so there will be room to run a vacuum cleaner under the bookcase. Mark the bottom of the shelf dado at 4 in. and mark the top of the dado at $4\frac{5}{8}$ in. **(photo 1)**. Next, measure up 30 in. from the top edge of the first dado and then lay out the location of the second shelf dado **(photo 2)**. Finally, lay out the top shelf 30 in. above the middle shelf.

Align the jig. Place the jig (see Build Your Skills on the facing page) over the case side, aligning the groove in the jig with the layout marks on the side of the case **(photo 3)**, then clamp the workpiece and jig to the bench **(photo 4)**.

T-Mac Tip

Make sure to put the side of the case on a sacrificial piece of wood before clamping it to the bench. This way, when the router bit exits the work, it won't cause any tearout on the face side of the bookcase.

Set the bit depth. Using a combination square, set the depth of the router bit at $\frac{1}{8}$ in. **(photo 5)**.

Make the cut. Wearing ear and eye protection, as well as a dust mask, cut the dadoes across the side of the case in two passes **(photo 6)**.

Safety First

Whenever making an adjustment to a power tool, be sure the tool is unplugged.

Case Work at the Fuller Craft Museum

An engaging exhibit at the Fuller Craft Museum in Brockton, Massachusetts, aptly titled "Furniture Divas," features some outstanding work by women furniture makers and demonstrates just how imaginative case work can be.

Some of the work is functional and some is purely sculptural, but all of it is beautifully done. Included in the installation is "Hope by Hope," by Sylvie Rosenthal, a nonfunctional sculpture that plays on the form of the traditional hope chest (center photo at left).

Also on display is a chest designed and built by Kristina Madsen, which is completely functional (photo below). Madsen's work is often characterized by intricate relief carving, a technique she learned from master carvers in Fiji. Adding interest and curiosity about the construction is the finish, which obscures which kind of joinery was used to build the case.

Another functional piece in the collection, titled "Dahlia," was designed and built by Jenna Goldberg. Goldberg

got into woodworking after a career in illustration and design. Her background really shows in both the carved exterior and silk-screened and painted interior of this cabinet (photos above). The corners of this case are mitered and reinforced with floating tenons.

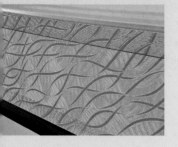

Above and right: Part of the "Furniture Divas" exhibit at The Fuller Craft Museum in Brockton, Massachusetts.

Above: Jenna Goldberg's cabinet has a silk-screened and painted interior.

Making the mortises

Lay out the mortises. The mortises are 2 in. wide. The outermost mortises begin 1 in. in from the edge, and there's a 2-in. space between the outer mortises and the one in the center. The locations for the mortises can be marked directly on the jig (**photo 1**). You also can lay out the mortise locations on the workpiece itself, although that's not absolutely necessary (**photo 2**).

Mark the router. On the side of the router, make reference marks for both edges of the bit (**photo 3**). Aligning those marks with the marks on the jig will ensure that you start and stop the mortises at the correct locations (**photo 4**).

Make the cuts. Don't try to cut the mortises in one single pass. It's better to make two or three passes, locking down the router at each depth (**photo 5**).

T-Mac Tip

Routing all that material will produce a lot of chips and dust. If possible, connect your router to a shop vacuum.

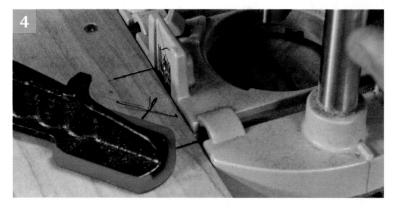

Square up the mortises. The router bit leaves rounded ends on the mortises (**photo 6**). If you left them like that, it would make creating the tenons extremely challenging. I chose to square off the mortises using a square to mark the ends of each one (**photo 7**).

Chop out the waste. With a wide bench chisel, begin working on the side walls of the mortises where the curve starts (**photo 8**). But don't put your chisel all the way into the corner because it will probably drift past the end of the mortise. Instead, work up to the corner slowly so that the last cut slices through all of the remaining wood fiber cleanly.

Work halfway then flip the board over. Start on the outside face of the side piece and chop halfway through the thickness of the board. Next, flip the board over and chop through the remaining thickness, creating four clean, crisp corners in each mortise (**photo 9**). If you try to go all the way through from one side, it may not be even on the flip side, and you run the risk of tearing out some of the fibers around the edge of the mortise.

Finish with the end grain. Once the side walls have been cleaned up, finish by squaring up the ends of the mortises with a ½-in. chisel (**photo 10**).

Sides and shelves

Lay out the rabbets. The back boards are set into a rabbet running the full length of the sides (**photo 1**). The rabbet is 9/16 in. wide (just a bit more than the 1/2-in.-thick back board) and 7/16 in. deep.

Cut the rabbets with a stack dado. One of the easiest ways to cut the rabbets is on a tablesaw with a stack dado set. Set up the dado at 5/8 in. and bury 1/16 in. of it in a sacrificial fence attached to your rip fence (**photo 2**). Once the blade has been set to its proper height and depth, you're ready to make some cuts (**photo 3**). Remember to cut both pieces, keeping in mind that there is a left and a right side of your project and the rabbets are positioned on the inside back edges.

To make the shelves, start by choosing the location and orientation of each of the fixed shelves, and mark them so they don't get mixed up. The shelves should be milled to just over 5/8 in. and fitted to the dadoes with a bench plane.

Mark the tenons. Set a shelf into its dado and tap it until it's fully seated (**photo 4**). Flip the assembly on its side and mark the tenons directly through the mortises (**photo 5**).

Saw to the shoulder line. Remove the shelf, then square the lines across the ends down to the shoulder line on each side; be sure you clearly mark the areas to be removed. The shoulder line should be drawn or knifed so it will allow the tenons to come completely through the side and stick out just a little bit. Use a handsaw to cut the shoulder line. Remember to stay outside the lines (**photo 6**).

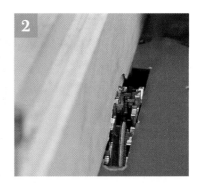

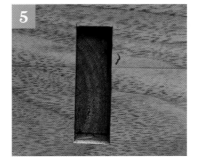

Remove the waste. Material between the sawkerfs can be removed on the tablesaw with a stack dado. Hold the shelves upright against the miter gauge and cut away the waste **(photo 7).** Clean up any roughness at the bench with a sharp chisel.

Dry-fit the shelves. Fit the tenons to their mortises **(photo 8).** If the fit is too tight, remove the shelf and look for areas where the wood fibers have been bruised or compressed. Shave these areas with a chisel until the shelf can go all the way in. Remember to place scrap wood under the side you're working on so the tenons can go completely through.

Flare the mortises. The ends of the tenons will be spread outward slightly with thin wedges to lock the shelves in place. To give the tenons room to expand, you'll need to flare the outer edges of the mortises. Make a knife line about $1/16$ in. away from the top and bottom of each mortise **(photo 9).** Then use a chisel to cut away the waste, working inward about half the thickness of the side **(photo 10).**

Kerf the tenons. Cut sawkerfs about $1/8$ in. from each face of the shelf on every tenon about half the thickness of the side case. Also, cut wedges for each of these kerfs. Trim the wedges so they are the same width as the tenons—that should be 2 in., but it may vary. Check each one.

Assembly. Glue all of the joints on one side of the case, inserting wedges as you go **(photo 11),** and clamp the case together with the other side dry. Make sure to drive both wedges in each tenon simultaneously. Check that the case is square. After a half hour, glue and wedge the other side.

Add the back. Mill the boards for the back to 1/2 in. thick and rabbet the edges as shown in the drawing on p. 149. During installation, keep the boards 1/4 in. apart using spacers to allow room for seasonal movement **(photo 12).**

Drill the shelf pin holes. Lay out the locations for the pin holes, 1 in. back from the front edge of the case and 1 in. in from the back rabbets. The holes can be drilled 2 in. apart. Make a stop block for the drill by drilling a hole in a block of wood. Only 7/16 in. of the bit should pop through the block.

Fit the shelves. Cut the shelves to length so they are about 1/8 in. shorter than the inside dimension of the case. Trim them to width—they should be 3/16 in. narrower than the depth of the case. Seat each shelf on a set of pins and trace the outlines of the pins on the bottom of the shelf. Chop out a 1/8-in.-deep mortise on the bottom of each shelf for the pins **(photo 13).**

Finishing up

After cleaning up any glue residue and sanding all surfaces, apply a coat of boiled linseed oil to the walnut to bring out the darkness of the wood. I did not use it on the maple because I wanted to keep that as light and natural looking as possible. After allowing the oil to dry, apply several coats of lacquer, sanding in between with 320-grit paper, and then finish up with steel wool and a coat of clear wax.

DESIGN Options

YOU CAN MAKE THIS BOOKCASE your own by introducing another shape on the top and bottom of the side pieces. You can try various profiles by outlining them with black electrical tape—it helps to visualize how they might look. A simple curve at the top of the case gives the piece an entirely different look.

POTTING STATION

Ripping Stock with a Circular Saw

This potting station makes a great project for anyone with a gardener in the family. It's designed to hold all your gardening needs, from potting soil to pots and fertilizer. In the top of the work surface, $1\frac{1}{4}$-in. holes allow soil and debris to be swept down into plastic bins below.

I made this potting station from western red cedar, a West Coast species that's naturally resistant to insects and inclement weather, which means the finish could be anything—from paint or stain to nothing at all. If left unfinished, the wood will turn a beautiful silvery gray.

One thing that makes this project a little different from building furniture is that tolerances don't have to be nearly as tight. The bench will be left outside in the elements, and the wood will move around, so there's no need to be quite as fussy as you need to be with the other projects in this book.

Another appealing aspect of this potting station is that it requires only a few tools—not much more than a circular saw and a cordless drill. You can set up shop in your yard or driveway with a temporary bench made from a sheet of plywood and a couple of sawhorses. Construction is also very simple. Pieces are simply cut to length and width and assembled with galvanized deck screws. There's no complex joinery involved, so it goes together very quickly and makes a perfect weekend project.

Potting Station

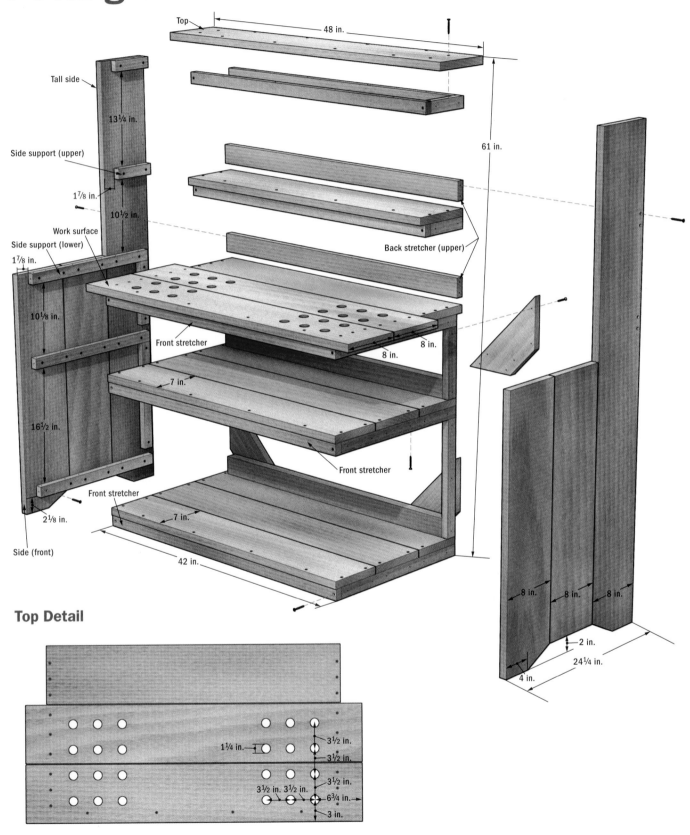

Top

48 in.

Tall side

13¼ in.

61 in.

Side support (upper)

1⅞ in.

10½ in.

Work surface

Back stretcher (upper)

Side support (lower)

1⅞ in.

10⅛ in.

8 in.

8 in.

Front stretcher

7 in.

16½ in.

Front stretcher

2⅛ in.

Front stretcher

Side (front)

7 in.

42 in.

8 in.   8 in.   8 in.

2 in.

24¼ in.

4 in.

Top Detail

3½ in.

1¼ in.

3½ in.

3½ in.

3½ in. 3½ in.

6¾ in.

3 in.

MATERIALS LIST/ROUGH MILL

PART	# OF PIECES	LENGTH (IN.)	WIDTH (IN.)	THICKNESS (IN.)	WOOD	NOTES
Tall Sides	2	61	8½	1⅛	Primary	
Sides (Front)	2	34¼	8½	1⅛	Primary	
Sides (Middle)	2	32¼	8½	1⅛	Primary	
Side Supports (Long)	6	22⅜	2	1⅛	Primary	
Shelves (Narrow)	4	43	7½	1⅛	Primary	
Shelves (Wide)	4	43	7½	1⅛	Primary	
Work Surfaces	2	49	8½	1⅛	Primary	
Top	1	49	8½	1⅛	Primary	
Front Stretchers	5	43	2	1⅛	Primary	
Back Stretchers (Upper)	2	43	3	1⅛		
Back Stretchers (Lower)	2	41	3	1⅛		
Vertical Braces (Long)	2	16½	2	1⅛		
Vertical Braces (Short)	2	10⅛	2	1⅛		
Corner Braces	4	16¾	5½	1⅛		
Screws	174					#8 x 1⅝-in. galvanized deck screws

TOOL LIST

POWER TOOLS
Circular saw
Cordless drill

HAND TOOLS
Combination square
Locking pliers
Measuring tape

Stock preparation

For this project, all you have to do is go to the lumberyard and buy the stock and get to work. There's no rough or finish milling involved.

When selecting stock, look for straight pieces. A very slight bow won't be a problem, but avoid any material that's twisted or badly cupped. It's not necessary to have perfectly clear stock, either. You can buy material with one good face and put the side with knots or other imperfections where they are less visible.

Western red cedar is an excellent choice because of its outdoor durability, but it can be a little pricey. Depending on where you live, you may be able to find locally harvested wood that's also naturally resistant to weather and insects at a lower price.

Cutting parts to length

Set up shop. A simple work station is about all you're going to need for this project (**photo 1**). You can set up in your garage, the driveway, or even in the yard, provided you're not too far from a source of power. The entire project is made from ten 8-ft. 1x8s.

Cut the pieces to length. The first step is to cut your pieces to length using a circular saw and a square. All you have to do to get a good cut is hold the square firmly against the edge of the board and use it as a guide for the shoe of the circular saw (**photo 2**). Start by squaring one end (**photo 3**) and plan your cuts to make the most of the material.

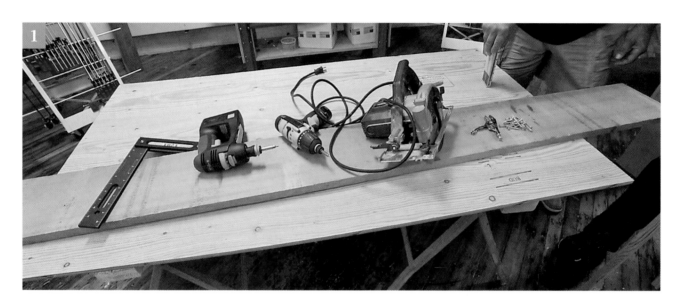

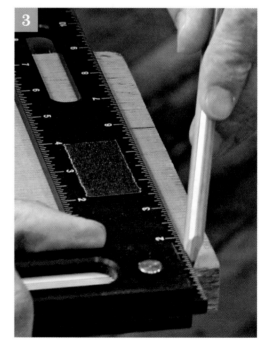

When cutting boards to length, you can hang one end over the bench (just be sure to support the offcut), or you can put the board on a couple of cauls to keep it off the work surface and clamp it in position (**photo 4**). You can also hold the piece down with your knee and free-hand the cut (**photo 5**). Just make sure your body is not directly behind the saw in case the piece kicks back.

Cut out the feet. Because the sides are so wide, it's a good idea to cut out feet at the bottom so the potting station can sit flat on uneven ground.

Lay out the feet. With the three pieces cut for one side, lay them out on the bench and mark a diagonal on the two outside pieces, starting 2 in. up and going over 4 in. to about the midpoint of each board (**photo 6**).

Safety First

Always wear ear and eye protection whenever you work around power tools. That's especially important when using a circular saw. The chips can really fly.

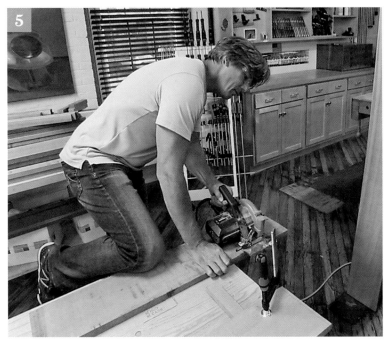

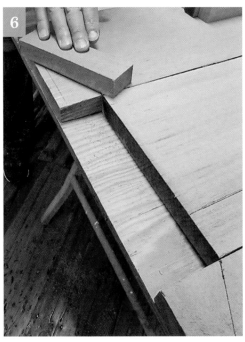

Ripping Stock without a Tablesaw

This project includes a number of narrow pieces of material that are used for cleats and stretchers. When you're in a fully equipped shop, ripping strips out of wide stock is no problem because you probably have a tablesaw.

When you are in the field, there is a simple way to accomplish the same thing. Mark the width of the strip, align the circular saw to the mark, and hold your finger against the edge of the board as a guide **(photo 1).** While this method works, you'll also get plenty of splinters in your finger when doing it that way.

A better way is to use a pair of locking pliers for your finger. Start by marking the width of the strip on the edge of the board **(photo 2).** Cut along the line for several inches, using your index finger as a guide for the saw **(photo 3).**

Stop the saw, leave it in the kerf, and lock the pliers on the shoe of the saw so the pliers are snug to the edge of the board **(photo 4).** Now you can easily complete the cut.

Assembling the sides

The sides are held together with three cleats, each 21⅜ in. long and 1½ in. wide. Two shorter cleats screwed to the tall side piece support the upper shelf and the top.

Lay out the sides. Lay out the three pieces for a side on the bench (good side down) and mark the location of the three longer cleats. The bottom cleat starts at 2⅛ in. up from the bottom (**photo 1**). The second cleat is placed 16½ in. above the first, allowing plenty of room for the plastic tubs. The top of the third cleat is aligned with the tops of the two outer boards.

The cleat doesn't span the full width of the side. It stops 1 in. from the back edge (**photo 2**), providing room for a brace, and it's just under 2 in. from the front edge, allowing for a stretcher across the front and a slight overhang for the shelf.

Attach the cleats. Place the cleats on the layout lines and screw them to the outermost board with two screws (**photo 3**). Leave a small space between the other two boards by using screws to form the gap (**photo 4**), then drive screws through the cleat into all three boards. Because the wood is so soft, you won't need to drill pilot holes, but keep the screws at least 1 in. away from the ends of the cleats to prevent splitting.

Screw in the short cleats at the top of the long side piece, this time with the back of the cleats flush with the back edge of the side (**photo 5**). Repeat the process for the other side.

A Pro-Style Potting Station

A potting station with a shelf over the main work area holds tools and supplies.

This project can trace its roots to the industrial-sized potting stations you'd find at a big greenhouse, like those at the Massachusetts Horticultural Society in Wellesley, Massachusetts.

David Fiske, the Gardens Curator, showed us what goes into a well-designed potting station. This includes a shelf over the worktable that holds the many supplies gardeners need—tools, gloves, tags, pots, and the like (photo at left).

The huge work surface has room enough for potting material and plants that need transplanting, like the impatiens shown below. Fiske is putting them into larger pots with a soil-less mixture of peat moss, perlite, vermiculite, and cooked bark.

Although the potting station we're building is a lot smaller, it has many of the same features as the ones at Mass Hort and will be just as useful.

Our potting station mimics the one at Mass Hort Society.

A large work area allows for repotting plants.

Adding the shelves

Some of the shelves are 42 in. long and others are 48 in. long. You'll get two shelves per 8-ft. board regardless of length because the planks actually measure 8 ft. 1 in. or 8 ft. 2 in. Start by cutting six of the 8-ft. planks in half. This will give you two square ends, which you can use as your reference edge when measuring and marking the shelves. As you cut the planks, keep all of the squared ends together, which will make cutting the shelves more efficient.

Cut the shelves. Cut the shelves to length, three at 48 in. and eight at 42 in. (**photo 1**).

Rip to width. The front and back boards on the lower shelves are 7 in. wide. The rest are 8 in. wide. Rip the four planks you'll need, using a circular saw and the locking pliers as a guide (**photo 2**).

Assemble the station. Start with the 8-in.-wide board on the bottom shelf and align it with the two center pieces on the sides. Screw the shelf to the cleats on both sides (**photo 3**). Add the middle piece of the center shelf (**photo 4**). At this point, the potting station should be relatively stable and able to stand on its own. Continue adding the rest of the shelves, using two screws per board at each connection.

Finally, add the 48-in.-long boards for the work surface. They should overhang each side by 2 in. Use three screws per board at each connection.

Adding the stretchers

All of the shelves, along with the top and the work surface, have stretchers underneath the front edge. Front and upper back stretchers are the same length as the shelves.

Screw in the front stretchers. Screw the stretchers to the front ends of the side cleats. Try to keep the screws 1 in. away from the ends, and avoid splitting the stretchers by driving in the screws at an angle (**photo 1**). In addition, drive several screws through both the top and the shelves and into the stretchers (**photo 2**).

T-Mac Tip

Sometimes two pieces of wood will be held slightly apart when you drive in a screw. If that happens, try backing out the screw just a bit and then driving it in again. That should do the trick.

Add stretchers in back. Add stretchers across the back to keep things from falling off the shelves and also to stiffen and strengthen the potting station. On the top shelves, hold the stretchers off the shelves by 1 in. and screw them in through the sides (**photo 3**).

Reinforce the lower half. The bottom of the potting station also gets stretchers, but first you need to add vertical cleats to the sides to provide a place to attach the corner brackets (**photo 4**). You then add the horizontal stretchers between these cleats. To attach them, run screws up through the bottom of the shelf and into the edge of the stretchers.

Make and install the brackets.
The potting station gets a lot of stability from the corner brackets that are screwed onto the back. They are 15³⁄₄ in. long with a 45-degree angle cut on each end. To get the most of your material, nest the pieces as you lay them out on the board **(photo 5)**. Screw them into the back so the bottom edge is flush with the bottom of the shelf **(photo 6)**.

Drill the holes for the soil grate. Lay out the grid for the holes on the work surface. The 1¹⁄₄-in.-dia. holes are 3¹⁄₂ in. on center. The center of the first hole on each side is 6³⁄₄ in. in from the end and 3 in. in from the front edge. Now drill out the holes **(photo 7)**. Other than buying a couple of plastic bins, the project is complete.

METRIC EQUIVALENTS

Inches	Centimeters	Millimeters	Inches	Centimeters	Millimeters
1/8	0.3	3	13	33.0	330
1/4	0.6	6	14	35.6	356
3/8	1.0	10	15	38.1	381
1/2	1.3	13	16	40.6	406
5/8	1.6	16	17	43.2	432
3/4	1.9	19	18	45.7	457
7/8	2.2	22	19	48.3	483
1	2.5	25	20	50.8	508
1 1/4	3.2	32	21	53.3	533
1 1/2	3.8	38	22	55.9	559
1 3/4	4.4	44	23	58.4	584
2	5.1	51	24	61.0	610
2 1/2	6.4	64	25	63.5	635
3	7.6	76	26	66.0	660
3 1/2	8.9	89	27	68.6	686
4	10.2	102	28	71.1	711
4 1/2	11.4	114	29	73.7	737
5	12.7	127	30	76.2	762
6	15.2	152	31	78.7	787
7	17.8	178	32	81.3	813
8	20.3	203	33	83.8	838
9	22.9	229	34	86.4	864
10	25.4	254	35	88.9	889
11	27.9	279	36	91.4	914
12	30.5	305			

INDEX